Washington Baird

The Confederate Spelling Book

Washington Baird

The Confederate Spelling Book

ISBN/EAN: 9783337372354

Printed in Europe, USA, Canada, Australia, Japan

Cover: Foto ©Thomas Meinert / pixelio.de

More available books at **www.hansebooks.com**

SPELLING BOOK:

ed according to Act of Congress, in the year 1864, by
WASHINGTON BAIRD,
rk's office of the District Court of the Confederate States,

INTRODUCTION.

In presenting to the Public this Elementary work for the use of the Families and Schools of our rising and glorious Confederacy, it is the duty of the Author to make the following explanatory and apologetic statements.

Nothing was farther from his mind than the thought of preparing such a work. The suggestions of friends, the extreme necessities of our beleaguered Confederacy, and the great importance of providing an immediate supply of such works on our own soil, have led to this attempt.

In the preparation of the work, the Author has deviated from all other plans. And yet this was not done from disrespect of any other authors, nor from any desire to innovate. Adaptation to our wants, as a people, and the securing of the highest good to the children and youth of our country, were his only motives.

Any great variety of suitable school books cannot, at once, be prepared and published. "FEW AND GOOD," should be our motto. The fact also is, that under the old dynasty, we had "series" after "series" of books *in the same department of instruction*, vastly beyond what was needed. A series of *five* or *six* READERS, for example, is an extravagance which should be avoided.

The great importance of *spelling*, no one can doubt. Long and thorough drilling should be given in that department. But spelling is a *task*, a *dull drudgery*, in which children seldom take any delight. It imparts no knowledge of Nature, of Art, or of Duty. It elicits no thought, and affords but little mental culture. Obviously, then, every lesson in spelling should have connected with it an exercise in *Reading* which is at once *pleasing* and *instructive*, affording food for thought, exercise for the several faculties of the mind, and calculated to produce a good *moral impression*. Moral principles and noble sentiments transcend all other qualities and attainments. And they should be largely and variously inculcated in the first books that are put into the hands of children and youth. The securing of these several ends has been kept steadily in view by the Author in the preparation of the whole work. It is known, also, that Rhyme and Poetry are eminently pleasing to children; and that they assist greatly the memory in treasuring up and retaining knowledge. And yet, strange to say, there is not a line of poetry in Webster's Spelling Book—the one in which most of the present generation have been instructed! - The moral also is a scarce article! The present work abounds in useful, and especially in *moral* instruction—a large portion of which is in choice poetry. Fables also are largely employed; Proverbs and Anecdotes are introduced. An effort is made to give an impulse to the mind toward many departments of knowledge. Its expanding powers are exercised in various apartments of Nature. Some of the reading lessons are of thrilling interest. " Past wrecks give fearful warnings." Hence the results of " Defective Education" are shown in ludicrous and appalling lights—admonitory against similar "*breakers*." An extended list of " prefixes" and " suffixes" is also added—showing the true import of our compound words, on principles easily understood and remembered.

Most of the reading lessons are simple and easy; but some of them are intended only for advanced pupils. The reasons for the introduction of the latter, will be apparent. The Spelling Book is commonly laid aside too soon. It should be the main book until a thorough mastery is obtained over *all* the departments of spelling. Hence reading lessons of corresponding character should be annexed or interspersed. This work is so arranged as to supply the want of the first two Readers in most of the other "series," as well as afford all needful exercises in spelling. On going through it each time, a higher mastery will be obtained over the more difficult parts. New food for thought will be found, as each field is again explored. Those pupils who can read well all the lessons which it contains, can read any thing else. Economy, Utility and Convenience are, therefore, combined in having *one* book instead of *three* or *four*, as was the case under the old system.

Should a PRIMER, containing a greater variety of easy spelling and reading lessons for *beginners*, be found necessary, the Author will take pleasure in preparing one. He intends also to prepare two Readers for advanced classes, the *latter* containing exercises also in Elocution. Thus the *three* works may suffice for the whole course of both spelling and reading, even in our higher schools.

In some elementary works many pages are occupied with elaborate treatises on the "Sounds of the Letters of the Alphabet." So far as *pupils* are concerned, this is useless. Those sounds can be learned only from the living Instructor. Teachers, in our day, are supposed to understand the pronunciation of their own mother tongue. To those engaged in that important and noble calling, the Author having given the *accent* and the *syllabification* of the words in the regular spelling lessons—confidently and cheerfully entrusts the whole business of instructing from the work, as now prepared. Observation and experience may indicate future changes and improvements. W. B.

THE ALPHABET.

The Alphabet of the English Language consists of twenty-six letters. Of these, *a, e, i, o,* and *u* are vowels, having distinct sounds of their own. All the other letters are consonants, sounding only in connection with the vowels; *w* and *y* are vowels when they end words and syllables. When they precede vowels sounded in the same syllable with themselves, they are consonants. Letters, as regards *form* and *size*, are divided into Capitals and small letters, Italics and Roman letters:

ROMAN.		ITALIC.		ROMAN.	
A	a	*A*	*a*	L	l
B	b	*B*	*b*	P	p
C	c	*C*	*c*	N	n
D	d	*D*	*d*	R	r
E	e	*E*	*e*	Z	z
F	f	*F*	*f*	Q	q
G	g	*G*	*g*	M	m
H	h	*H*	*h*	Y	y
I	i	*I*	*i*	K	k
J	j	*J*	*j*	C	c
K	k	*K*	*k*	J	j
L	l	*L*	*l*	F	f
M	m	*M*	*m*	B	b
N	n	*N*	*n*	U	u
O	o	*O*	*o*	A	a
P	p	*P*	*p*	G	g
Q	q	*Q*	*q*	X	x
R	r	*R*	*r*	D	d
S	s	*S*	*s*	W	w
T	t	*T*	*t*	S	s
U	u	*U*	*u*	I	i
V	v	*V*	*v*	T	t
W	w	*W*	*w*	V	v
X	x	*X*	*x*	O	o
Y	y	*Y*	*y*	H	h
Z	z	*Z*	*z*	E	e

FIGURES.

1   2   3   4   5   6   7   8   9   10.

DOUBLE LETTERS.

EXERCISE UPON THE LETTERS.

The following is an exercise for beginners upon the *several kinds of letters*, as presented by repetitions of the same words. It may be either spelled or read. Its utility, as an *exercise*, is obvious.

BE	JUST	AND	WIN	THE	PRIZE.
Be	just	and	win	the	prize.
Be	*just*	*and*	*win*	*the*	*prize.*

BE	KIND	AND	GOOD	TO	ALL.
Be	kind	and	good	to	all.
Be	*kind*	*and*	*good*	*to*	*all.*

LOVE	GOD	WITH	ALL	THE	HEART.
Love	God	with	all	the	heart.
Love	*God*	*with*	*all*	*the*	*heart.*

O	QUIT	EACH	WAY	OF	SIN.
O	quit	each	way	of	sin.
O	*quit*	*each*	*way*	*of*	*sin.*

FROM	GOD	ALL	GOOD	EXPECT.
From	God	all	good	expect.
From	*God*	*all*	*good*	*expect.*

ON DOUBLE LETTERS.

Fin, fill, flint, luff, muffin.
Scuffle, fish, flesh, flippant.
Whiffle, abb, ebb, egg.
Off, beep, boon, bill, whiff.
Purr, runnion, puss, butt.
Add, Aaron, apple, otter.

LESSON I.

Words and Syllables of Two Letters.

NOTE.—C sounds like *k* before a, o and u; like *s* before *e*, *i* and *y*.

ba	be	bi	bo	bu	by	ab	eb
ib	ob	ub	ca	ce	ci	co	cu
cy	da	de	di	do	du	dy	ad
ed	id	od	ud	fa	fe	fi	fo
fu	fy	af	ef	if	of	uf	ha
he	hi	ho	hu	hy	ja	je	ji
jo	ju	jy	ka	ke	ki	ko	ku

be	by	me	me	by	it	on	an	ox
he	at	it	it	by	me	ox	on	it

LESSON II.

la	le	li	lo	lu	ly	al	el
il	ol	ul	ma	me	mi	mo	mu
my	am	em	im	om	um	na	ne
ni	no	nu	ny	an	en	in	on
un	pa	pe	pi	po	pu	py	ap
ep	ip	op	up	ra	re	ri	ro
ru	ry	ar	er	ir	or	ur	uz

so	I	am	in	it	is	go	to	it
am	I	so?	is	it	in?	it	to	go

LESSON III.

sa	se	si	so	su	sy	as	cs
is	os	us	ys	ta	te	ti	to
tu	ty	at	et	it	ot	ut	va
ve	vi	vo	vu	vy	av	iv	ov
uv	wa	we	wi	wo	ax	ex	ix
ox	ux	ya	ye	yo	za	ze	zi
zo	zu	zy	az	ez	iz	oz	uz

as it is
sit by us
so do we
sea the ox
do it now

so be it
by us sit
we do so
he is fat
now do it

up to it
to go at
do it so
to go in
or go by

LESSON IV.

Words and Syllables of Three Letters.

bad	bag	cab	ban	bap	bat
cad	dag	dab	can	cap	cat
dad	fag	gab	dan	dap	fat
gad	gag	nab	fan	gap	hat
had	hag	pab	man	hap	mat
mad	nag	rab	pan	map	pat
pad	rag	sab	ran	sap	rat
sad	tag	tab	tan	tap	sat

I am to be up   he is to go in   an ox is by me
up I am to be   in he is to go   by me is an ox
if we do go up!   is it my cat, pa?   my cap, it is so!

LESSON V.

bam	lax	ben	bed	bet	bin
cam	tax	den	fed	get	din
dam	wax	fen	led	let	fin
ham	bex	hen	ned	met	gin
jam	dex	men	red	net	pin
ram	sex	pen	wed	pet	sin
yam	vex	ten	zed	yet	win

The cat has got a rat,   The hen sits by the tree,
How very nice and fat;   The chick-ens too you see;
The dog lies on the hay,   The bird sits on the limb,
The pup-pies by him stay.   And sings its pret-ty hymn.

LESSON VI.

bla	ble	bli	blo	blu	bly
fla	fle	fli	flo	flu	fly
gla	gle	gli	glo	glu	gly
pla	ple	pli	plo	plu	ply
rha	rhe	rhi	rho	rhu	rhy
sla	sle	sli	slo	slu	sly
tra	tre	tri	tro	tru	try

Here is my lit-tle box, The pig is in his pen,
And there the old fat ox; See, too, the lit-tle wren;
O! my old map is wet, Now I've got a fire bug,
A new one I will get. I'll put him in the jug.

LESSON VII.

bra	bre	bri	bro	bru	bry
cra	cre	cri	cro	cru	cry
dra	dre	dri	dro	dru	dry
fra	fre	fri	fro	fru	fry
gra	gre	gri	gro	gru	gry
pra	pre	pri	pro	pru	pry
tra	tre	tri	tro	tru	try

The old man wears a wig, The bee is on the wing,
And feeds his fat-ted pig; Be-ware his cru-el sting;
The wasp now makes his nest, Now ope this i-ron box,
He is a hor-rid pest. And see my pret-ty fox.

LESSON VIII.

pha	phe	phi	pho	phu	phy
sha	she	shi	sho	shu	shy
bug	dug	hug	jug	mug	rug
bot	cot	dot	hot	mot	sot
bit	fit	hit	kit	pit	sit
dip	hip	lip	rip	sip	tip
bob	cob	fob	job	rob	sob

The cat has shut her eye, The ox now eats his corn,
Now I can eat a pie; A fly sits on his horn;
I see the old fat ox, O! put a-way the map,
Here lies my pret-ty fox. Now let us take a nap.

LESSON IX.

bog	dog	cog	fog	gog	log
bud	cud	dud	hud	mud	rud
big	fig	gig	hig	rig	wig
bum	gum	hum	mum	rum	sum
bub	cub	dub	hub	rub	tub
bun	dun	fun	gun	run	tun
bar	car	far	gar	mar	tar

The dog has got his meat,   The cat is on the log,
Come now and see him eat; She hiss-es at the dog;
O! see the pret-ty boy,   The fish swim in the sea,
He has a nice new toy.   A fish-er I would be.

LESSON X.

bay	day	gay	hay	lay	may
pay	ray	say	way	dew	few
hew	jew	mew	new	pew	tew
bod	cod	hod	nod	rod	sod
fop	hop	mop	pop	sop	top
bib	fib	nib	rib	sib	tib
spa	spe	spi	spo	spu	spy

The bee-tle now I spy,   I feed my pet on rice,
And see its lit-tle eye;   And keep him from the mice;
It sits upon the flow-er,   With-in his cage he sleeps,
With-in the sha-dy bow-er. Or thro' its bars he peeps.

LESSON XI.

Easy Words of Two Syllables.

di al	ga la	po em	pu ny	fi at
ty ro	la va	po et	ha zy	fu ry
he ro	ru in	du el	la zy	to ry
la va	vi al	na vy	la dy	ca to
pi ca	re al	ma zy	za ny	lu cy
so da	ri ot	bo ny	si zy	ro sy
so fa	bi as	po ny	ti dy	fu el
ha lo	di et	do zy	li my	fu my

The rain is fall-ing fast,   The calves now crop the grass,
The win-ter days are past;   And scam-per as we pass;
The birds are on the wing,   The lambs I love to see,
And O! how nice they sing.   And near them ever be.

LESSON XII.

bid	boy	bon	die	fix	ace
did	coy	con	fie	mix	age
hid	joy	don	hie	pix	ale
lid	roy	mon	lie	rix	ape
mid	toy	pon	pie	six	ate

lag	hem	caw	maw	cue	elk
sag	gem	daw	saw	due	ell
tag	cup	law	taw	hue	elm
wag	sup	paw	raw	rue	end

The e-vil way of sin   But take the up-ward track,
O! nev-er once be-gin;   And ne'er from it turn back,
Lest then you on-ward go   Then Heav-en will be your home
To pain and end-less wo;   For end-less years to come.

LESSON XIII.

Words of Four Letters.

bane	vane	bale	cope	bone	dire
cane	wane	gale	hope	cone	fire
fane	cave	hale	lope	lone	hire
lane	gave	kale	mope	tone	mire
mane	lave	male	pope	dive	sire
pane	nave	sale	rope	hive	tire
sane	save	tale	tope	rive	wire

To all be kind and true,   The moon is clear and bright,
No e-vil ev-er do;   The stars give light by night;
You must not work or play   And all the show-ers that fall
Up-on God's ho-ly day.   For grate-ful prais-es call.

LESSON XIV.

bake	bare	bent	fine	blot	bore
cake	care	cent	dine	clot	core
lake	dare	dent	line	glot	fore
make	fare	gent	mine	plot	gore
rake	hare	lent	nine	quot	lore
sake	mare	ment	pine	shot	more
take	pare	rent	tine	spot	sore
wake	tare	sent	wine	trot	tore

Take not God's name in vain,   Love God with all your heart,
Each sin will leave a stain;   From evil ways de-part;
God's ho-ly word is true,   Keep all God's laws in sight,
It tells you what to do.   And pray for guid-ing light.

LESSON XV.

dace	cage	code	bite	date	bile
face	gage	mode	cite	gate	file
lace	page	node	mite	hate	mile
mace	rage	rode	rite	late	pile
pace	sage	tone	site	mate	tile
race	wage	zone	zite	pate	wile
made	came	gore	cure	cape	fife
fade	dame	sore	lure	tape	life
jade	fame	tore	pure	nape	rife
wade	lame	wore	sure	rape	wife

All Na-ture's fresh and gay,
Come let us take our play;
How sweet-ly in the spring
The woods with music ring.

I love the thou-sand flow-ers,
And all the bloom-ing bow-ers;
But roses red and white—
They are my chief de-light.

LESSON XVI.

bold	best	bate	bolt	ball	crab
cold	lest	date	colt	call	drab
fold	nest	fate	dolt	fall	grab
gold	rest	gate	jolt	gall	blab
hold	test	hate	malt	hall	slab
mold	vest	mate	halt	pall	stab
sold	west	rate	roll	tall	crag
told	zest	sate	toll	wall	drag

O, come and see my top,
How it does spin and hop!
And then it *hums*, you see,
Like the pret-ty bee!
It is no com-mon toy,
It fills me full of joy!

And now it is my wish,
To catch a lit-tle fish;
I'll take my pole and hook
Down to the flow-ing brook,
I'll catch the lit-tle sin-ner,
And bring him home for din-ner.

We must either advance or go backward. If we are not learning, we are losing.

Idleness and want are twin sisters; and they always dwell together.

LESSON XVII.

THE SNAIL AND THE SHIP.

The snail lives in its shell,
I found it in the dell;
For house it can-not lack,
It bears one on its back.

The ships sail on the sea,
And there I like to be;
When high the wind doth rave,
And mount the foam-ing wave.

Words of Two Syllables, Accented on the First.

co pal	pe nal	to per	so ber	vo ter
do tal	ve nal	fo cal	ca per	ro ver
lo cal	re gal	sa vor	su ral	am ber
to tal	le gal	fe ver	sy ren	up per
ho ral	mo dal	lu nar	ci der	un der
vo cal	na sal	Ro man	la ver	o ver
fa tal	pa pal	hu man	vi per	o ral
na tal	po lar	pa gan	ca per	po ker
vi tal	so lar	Si mon	pa per	to ken
fi nal	fa vor	ni tre	pi per	bo lus

Be ev-er good and true,
Mind what you say and do;
God's word would make you wise,
Do not its truth de-spise.

Learn some-thing ev-e-ry day,
And ev-er watch and pray;
To run in ways of sin
O! nev-er once be-gin.

HOW I LOVE.

How I love my tender mother,
   How I love my father dear;
How I love my little brother,
   And my gentle sister here:
They are all both kind and true,
And they dearly love me too.

Be my neighbor proud or lowly,
   He shall my affection share;
Be he sinful, be he holy,
   He may claim my earnest prayer:
Let me not unfeeling prove,
Nor myself too dearly love.

But of all affection given,
  God on high demands the most;
God the Father in the heaven,
  God the Son, and Holy Ghost:
Three in one, and One in three,
  Be thou all in all to me.

LESSON XVIII.

bind	band	bame	bate	bank
find	hand	came	date	hank
hind	land	dame	late	lank
mind	mand	game	mote	rank
rind	pand	lame	note	sank
wind	rand	name	pote	tank
hove	sand	same	rote	bulk
rove	ripe	tame	sote	hulk
wove	type	fame	vote	sulk

A SECRET.

THE LITTLE NESTS.

There is a se-cret I would like
The lit-tle *girls* to know;
But I won't tell a sin-gle boy—
They rob the birds' nests so.

We have four pret-ty lit-tle nests,
We watch them with great care;
Full fif-ty eggs are in this tree—
Don't tell the boys they're there!

Joe Thomp-son rob-bed the nests, last year,
And year be-fore, Tom Brown;
I'll tell it, loud as I can sing,
To ev-e-ry one in town.

LESSON XIX.

STEALING.

"Does Har-ry Flint steal apples?"

"No! nor any thing else. He would as soon cut off his own right hand as to steal. When he was a child his moth-er taught him this les-son:

    "In God's sight, it is a sin,
    To steal a pen-ny or a pin."

He has re-mem-ber-ed that les-son to this day. In-deed he nev-er will for-get it. He acts on that prin-ci-ple in al that he does; and eve-ry bod-y hon-ors him for it."

"Well, then, I want to em-ploy him," said Mr. Wil son. "But, as for Tom Sands, I would not let him com in-side of my door, he is such a liar and thief."

Words of Five Letters.

block	brays	barns	bangs	barks
clock	frays	carns	fangs	harks
flock	grays	darns	gangs	larks
smock	slays	tarns	hangs	marks
stock	stays	yarns	pangs	parks
crock	sways	farms	tangs	bakes
frock	prays	harms	bores	cakes
whelp	quays	brags	cores	lakes
yelps	plays	crags	sores	makes

LESSON XX.

BE WISE AND GOOD.

Oh! no, I'll nev-er be a fool,
For I will mind my books and school;
I'll learn of du-ty all I can,
And strive to be a use-ful man.
My fel-low pu-pils I will love,
And try to be like those a-bove.

caves	bites	bines	holes	bends
laves	cites	dines	moles	lends
waves	kites	fines	poles	sends
fades	mites	mines	soles	sakes
lades	rites	lines	lobes	wakes
rades	bides	pines	robes	pants
gales	hides	sines	notes	rants
sales	rides	tines	votes	hills
darts	nests	vines	hopes	mills
parts	pests	wines	ropes	pills

TIME.

Chil-dren sel-dom think of the value of time. But i is far bet-ter than gold. They should be care-ful to im prove it as it flies. The days of youth will soon pass a-way; and they will nev-er re-turn. Those who are i-dle in youth will re-gret it very much when they are old. Let all child-ren, then, take warn-ing; im-prove all their time, and do all their du-ty. Thus they will be both use-ful and hap-py.

LESSON XXI.

carts	falls	binds	books	feels
darts	balls	finds	cooks	heels
harts	calls	hinds	nooks	keels
marts	galls	kinds	looks	reels
parts	malls	minds	rooks	deeds
tarts	palls	winds	hooks	feeds
cents	wasps	bolts	cools	boots
rents	wands	colts	fools	coots
panes	warts	dolts	boons	hoots
vanes	warps	jolts	moons	roots

We love the lit-tle girls and boys,
And give them pret-ty toys.
The kit-tens go to bed,
When they, on milk, are fed.
The bird is on the tree,
And chirps its note for me.

Hear how the lit-tle lark
Flies up when it is dark!
He ris-es up on high
To car-rol in the sky,
Then down he comes, you see,
And sits be-neath the tree.

SPRING.

"Spring is com-ing, Spring is com-ing," said lit-tle An-nie, "for now the lit-tle snow-drops and the vi-o lets are be-gin-ning to peep through the green leaves. O, how glad I am; for soon the air will be fill-ed with sweet per-fume, and we shall have so ma-ny pret-ty flow-ers.

The mea-dows, then, will be cov-er-ed with fresh grass. The lit-tle lambs will de-light us with their sports, and the birds will fill the for-est with their cheerful notes. O, how de-light-ful Spring is!

MARINERS.

How cheer-y are the mar-i-ners,
Those lov-ers of the sea!
Their hearts are like the crest-ed waves,
As bound-ing and as free.

XXII.

brave	blame	blade	bride	spoke
crave	flame	glade	chide	smoke
grave	frame	shade	bribe	scope
shave	shame	grade	tribe	slope
slave	shape	spade	glide	grope
stave	grape	trade	slide	trope
brake	plate	shine	drove	grace
flake	state	swine	grove	place
shake	stake	twine	stove	brace
snake	drake	brine	snore	mange
spake	quake	trine	store	range

AGAINST QUARRELING AND FIGHTING.

Let dogs de-light to bark and bite,
  For 'tis their na-ture to;
Let bears and li-ons growl and fight,
  For God hath made them so.

But, child-ren, you should nev-er let
  Your an-gry pas-sions rise;
Your lit-tle hands were nev-er made
  To tear each other's eyes.

What-ev-er brawls dis-turb the street,
  There should be peace at home;
Where sis-ters dwell and broth-ers meet,
  Quar-rels should nev-er come.

LESSON XXIII.

HANDS.

"I have a pair of ti-ny hands,
They're lit-tle bits of things;
But moth-er says, that they were made
To serve the "king of kings."

bland	blank	crack	bring	clung
grand	crank	track	cling	flung
brand	drank	smack	fling	brick
stand	flank	slack	swing	stick
stamp	frank	stack	brink	trick
cramp	prank	quack	think	click

speck	small	bless	flush	blend
check	stall	dress	crush	spend
smell	crawl	chess	stock	bench
spell	yawl	press	clock	wench

THE LITTLE SPARROW.

Glad to see you, little bird,
'Twas your little chirp I heard;
What did you in-tend to say?
" Give me some-thing this cold day."

That I will, and plen-ty too;
All these crumbs I sav-ed for you;
Don't be fright-en-ed, here's a treat—
I will wait and see you eat.

LESSON XXIV.

MY LITTLE BODY.

My lit-tle body's very weak,
A fall or blow my bones might break;
The wa-ter soon might stop my breath,
The fire might close my eyes in death.

But God can keep me by his care,
To Him I'll say this lit-tle pray-er:
" O, God! from harm my body keep,
Both when I wake and when I sleep."

Words of Two Syllables, Accented on the Second.

a bate	be gin	de base	ra zee	re tire
a bide	be tide	de vote	re bate	se date
a bode	be lie	de cade	re late	so lace
a rise	be dim	de lude	re print	se cede
a rose	be mire	de nude	re mark	se cure
a dore	be side	de fame	re fine	se rene
a maze	de ride	de rive	re lume	se crete
a base	de note	de port	re cline	se vere
a like	de sire	de fy	re buke	se duce
a live	de pose	de ny	re vive	se clude

THE MODEL BOY.

Wil-liam is a good boy. See him yon-der in the field look-ing af-ter his fath-er's sheep. He has a lit-tle box in his hand full of salt. The sheep love to see him, for he al-ways has some-thing for them.

Now he is put-ting salt on a board. See how they come run-ning to him. They are glad to get it, and it is very good for them.

When the sheep stray off from home, he and the boy Ned get on their po-nies and hunt them up.

Wil-liam loves his moth-er, and al-ways does as she bids him. When she sends him on an er-rand, he nev-er plays by the way. When he goes to school, he tries to learn all his les-sons well; and when he is at home, he is al-ways try-ing to do some-thing use-ful. Eve-ry body loves him; and he will be a great and a good man some day.

PLAY.

Let your sports be gay, but kind;
Thus the bod-y helps the mind;
Earn-est plays, if not too long,
Make both mind and bod-y strong.

DUTIES.

Love God, who all your bless-ings gives,
With all your heart and mind;
And love your neigh-bor as your-self,
Be ev-er faith-ful, just and kind.

Deal with an-other as you'd have
An-other deal with you;
What you're un-will-ing to re-ceive,
Be sure you nev-er do.

LESSON XXV.

DIPHTHONGS AND DIGRAPHS.

A diphthong is a union of two vowels, both of which are sounded. As *oil, loud, proud*.

A digraph is the union of two vowels, of which only one is sounded. As s*e*a, p*e*ach, r*o*ad. The digraphs are marked with italics.

DIPHTHONGS.			DIGRAPHS.		
oil	our	bound	oar	load	coach
boil	sour	hound	soar	goad	poach
coil	awl	sound	roar	road	roach
toil	owl	growl	earn	toad	mails
moil	bout	prowl	learn	coat	pails
soil	lout	ounce	yearn	goat	sails

GOD OUR MAKER.

In six days God made the world, and all that is in it.

He made the sun to give light by day, and the moon and stars to shine by night.

The grass, the plants and the trees were made to a-dorn the earth, and give food to man and beast.

He made man in his own im-age, and placed him over all that He had made upon the earth.

When He had made all things He said they were very good.

We ought, then, to love God for what He had done for us. And we ought nev-er to do any thing bad in this good world which He has made for our use.

LESSON XXVI.
EVENING.

The day-light fades,
The evening shades
Are gathering round my *head;*
Father above,
I own the love
That smooths and guards my bed.

While Thou art near,
I need not fear
The gloom of mid-night's hour;
Dear Savior still,
From every ill,
Defend me with Thy power.

Pardon my sin,
And enter in,
And sanctify my heart,
Spirit Divine;
Oh! make me thine,
And ne'er from me depart.

In the following words, the vowel *a* of the digraph *ea* has no sound; and the *e* has the short sound of that letter, as in *met*.

bread	breath	earl	ear nest	feath er
head	death	pearl	ear ly	weath er
lead	earth	earn	earth ly	health y
read	dearth	learn	earth en	wealth y
stead	sweat	yearn	heav en	meas ure
tread	threat	cleanse	leav en	treas ure
dread	health	dreamt	clean ly	pleas ant
spread	wealth	meant	search ing	pleas ure
dead	stealth	realm	heav y	jeal ous
thread	breadth	breast	leath er	zeal ous

To God all hon-or give,
And to His glo-ry live.
Be love-ly in His eyes,
And then to Him a-rise.
Those who the Sa-vior love,
Shall reign with Him a-bove.

From ways of sin now cease,
And make with God your peace.
Man's body, tho' it dies,
Yet it a-gain shall rise.
Of all your words take care,
And nev-er lie nor swear.

EARLY PIETY.

Happy the child, whose tender years
  Receive instruction well,
Who hates the sinner's path, and fears
  The road that leads to hell.

"GOOD NIGHT."

At night my mother comes up stairs,
She comes to hear us say our prayers;
And while I'm sitting on her knee,
She always kiss-es little me.

Before she took away the light,
She tucked the blankets close and tight;
And round about my sleepy head,
She drew the curtains of the bed.

I saw her walk across the floor,
And softly close the nurse-ry door,
And then I called, with all my might,
"Good night, dear mamma, good night."

LESSON XXVII.

Words of Two Syllables, Accented on the First.

ma ker	gi ant	bi ter	i cy
na vy	ta ker	fri ar	la bel
ne gro	ti ger	cri er	li bel
sli my	pa cer	vi per	lu nar
fa vor	gro cer	ni tre	plu ral
me tre	wo ful	ro ver	fin ish
mo tive	fit ful	tro ver	hor rid
ze ro	fin ish	wa ver	sol id
tu lip	lin net	ca ger	dol lar
tu tor	mil let	pi lot	dan dy
ce dar	min ion	pli ant	dap ple
cra zy	mim ic	se ton	dor sal
tri al	mor al	li bel	ton sil
ru ler	mor tar	do nor	ton ic
ru ral	pot ter	fla vor	Lat in
pu pil	pil fer	ha ler	liv er
cru et	pup py	ha ter	liv id
cru el	pes ter	hu mid	lum ber
gru el	hat ter	tu mid	lub ber
vi tal	mat ter	i dol	ros in

LESSON XXVIII.

TOBACCO.

I'll never use tobacco, no!
  It is a filthy weed;
It never in my mouth shall go,
  Said little Robert Reed.

In the following words the *e* of the digraph has the first sound of *e*, as in *me*, and the other vowels are silent.

east	eat	eaves	ear	cream	bean
beast	beat	leaves	dear	dream	dean
least	feat	heaves	fear	fleam	lean
feast	heat	greaves	hear	gleam	mean
yeast	meat	weaves	shear	scream	wean
cease	neat	hears	blear	piece	glean
peace	seat	fears	clear	niece	fierce
lease	peat	gears	smear	liege	pierce
crease	treat	sears	near	siege	speak
grease	bleat	tears	rear	bleat	squeak
brief	meal	thief	drear	wheat	shriek
lief	neal	grief	year	beam	beach
ceil	peal	wield	spear	seam	leach
deal	seal	shield	bead	team	preach
heal	veal	field	lead	plead	reach
wheal	weal	yield	mead	knead	teach

"GOOD NIGHT."
[CONTINUED.]

I told you what I said to "ma,"
As she went back to sit with "pa;"
And now I wish to let you see
What it was she said to me:

That dear mam-ma! so sweet and mild,
I heard her say, "GOD BLESS MY CHILD;"
And al-ways when she goes a-way,
Those are the words we hear her say.

Oh! what a happy child am I,
When in my lit-tle crib I lie,
Blest by a ten-der moth-er's love,
And by the ho-ly God above.

NOAH AND THE NEW WORLD.

And Noah builded an altar unto the Lord, and took of every clean beast, and of every clean fowl, and offered burnt offerings on the altar. And the Lord smelled a sweet savor, and the Lord said in his heart, I will not again curse the ground any more for man's sake; for the imagination of man's heart is evil from his youth; neither will I smite every living thing any more as I have done.

While the earth remaineth, seed time and harvest, and cold and heat, and summer and winter, and day and night, shall not cease.

LESSON XXIX.

KINDNESS.

THE PET LAMB.

Mary had a little lamb,
  Its fleece was white as snow;
And ev-e-ry-where that Mary went
  The lamb was sure to go.

He went with her to school one day,
  That was against the rule;
It made the children laugh and play
  To see a lamb at school.

So the teacher turned him out,
  But still he lingered near,
And waited patiently about,
  Till Mary did appear.

And then he ran to her and laid
  His head upon her arm,
As if he said, "I'm not afraid,
  You'll keep me from all harm."

What makes the lamb love Mary so?
  The eager children cry;
"O! Mary loves the lamb, you know,"
  The teacher did reply.

" And you, each gentle animal
  To you, for life, may bind,
And make it follow at your will,
  If you are always kind."

B

Words of Two Syllables, Accented on the Second.

a base	a wake	com pare	ob late
a bate	a live	con nate	ad mire
a side	a like	col late	af ford
a pace	a tone	com pose	ad vise
a maze	a dore	con s me	as size
a wake	a bode	bap tize	il lume
a ware	a bide	com mode	at tune
ar rive	a cute	com pute	ac quire
ca jole	as size	com mune	ac cede
as pire	ma ture	com port	al lude
at tire	sa lute	com ply	al lure
ca nine	ac crue	com plete	ma ture

I went by the field of the slothful, and by the vineyard of the man void of understanding; and lo! it was all grown over with thorns, and nettles had covered the face thereof, and the stone wall thereof was broken down.

Then I saw and considered it well; I looked upon it and received instruction. Yet a little sleep, a little slumber, a little folding of the hands to sleep.

So shall thy poverty come as one that treveleth, and thy want as an armed man.—[*Solomon*.

LESSON XXX.
SWEAR NOT.

I must not use God's name in vain,
Or ever speak a word profane;
For those who learn to curse and swear,
The children of the Devil are:
My little lips, Oh, may they be
Attuned, O Lord, to honor Thee!

Words whose Meanings are Alike.

babe	child	harm	hunt	sack	bag
beak	bill	hurl	throw	loop	noose
bind	tie	flame	blaze	peak	point
bile	gall	heap	pile	pawn	pledge
brute	beast	hide	skin	bilge	leak

bond	deed	jest	joke	tine	prong
boon	gift	lad	boy	glade	lawn
bulb	root	maize	corn	pest	plague
bush	shrub	noun	name	poll	head
bulk	size	lout	clown	blank	void
cowl	hood	den	cave	crude	raw
dread	fear	rind	bark	fain	glad
fib	lie	space	room	prime	first
flesh	meat	staff	cane	calm	still
glebe	soil	stag	deer	bleak	cold
glee	fun	polt	blow	rope	cord
fume	smoke	guile	craft	lax	loose
flaw	crack	blotch	stain	vast	great

LITTLE FRED.

When little Fred was called to bed,
He always acted right;
He kissed mamma, and then papa,
And wished them both good night.

He made no noise, like naughty boys,
But softly up the stairs,
Directly went as he was sent,
And always said his prayers.

Then little Fred, all snug in bed,
Did gently go to sleep;
Nor did he ever lift his head,
Till day began to peep.

LESSON XXXI.

MORNING.

The morning bright,
With rosy light,
Hath waked me from my sleep,
Father! I own
Thy love alone
Thy little one doth keep.

All through the day,
O God I pray,
Be thou my guard and guide;
My sins forgive,
And let me live,
Dear Savior, near thy side.

Oh, make Thy rest,
Within my breast,
Great Spirit of all grace;
Make me like Thee,
Then shall I be
Prepared to see Thy face.

Words of Two Syllables, Accented on the First.

bla tant	blem ish	blis ter	fin ish
bla zon	bles sing	bliss ful	fen nel
clo ven	blus ter	blos som	fer ret
clo ver	blub ber	bow er	box er
car man	blun der	bow els	boy ish
car ver	blot ted	bran dy	cap tive
car nal	bran dish	can dy	cat tle
cor nish	bram ble	bro ken	cal ends
dis mal	cem ent	bro ker	can vass
dim ple	cen sus	cin der	clar et
hin der	cher ry	cir cle	cis tern
hun ter	cher ub	civ ic	cler gy
med al	dent ist	civ il	clin ic
men sal	dim ness	cav il	clos et

THE BLESSED.

Blessed are the poor in spirit; for their's is the kingdom of heaven.

Blessed are they that mourn; for they shall be comforted.

Blessed are the meek; for they shall inherit the earth.

Blessed are they who hunger and thirst after righteousness; for they shall be filled.

Blessed are the merciful; for they shall obtain mercy.

Blessed are the pure in heart; for they shall see God.

Blessed are the peace-makers.; for they shall be called the children of God.

Blessed are they who are persecuted for righteousness' sake; for their's is the kingdom of heaven.

Blessed are ye, when men shall revile you, and persecute you, and shall say all manner of evil against you falsely, for my sake.

Rejoice and be exceeding glad; for great is your reward in heaven; for so persecuted they the prophets who were before you.—*Bible.*

LESSON XXXII.

HOW TO ACT.

My books I must not tear or lose,
    But try to keep them clean and neat;
And vile bad words I must not use,
    Like those I hear when in the street.

And I must think of what I'm told,
    And as I'm bid must try to do;
I must not mock the lame or old,
    Nor should I say what is not true.

These are the things I ought to mind,
    And so I will, with all my might;
For I am sure that I shall find,
    I must be *loved*, if I do *right*.

Words of Five and Six Letters.

bonds	files	dates	crafts	blocks
ponds	miles	fates	drafts	clocks
cures	tiles	gates	grafts	docks
lures	gales	hates	shafts	flocks
tunes	tales	mates	rafts	locks
prunes	loads	pates	wafts	frocks
spoons	roads	rates	carps	mocks
moons	toads	states	harps	rocks

ACCENT means giv-ing great-er force of ut-ter-ance to some one syl-la-ble of a word than is giv-en to the others. The word "ar-ri-val" has the ac-cent on the *se-cond* syl-la-ble—rí—but the word "*ma-ker*" has it on the *first*—má-ker—not ma-ker. Your teach-er will ex-plain this to you, and give you ma-ny more ex-am-ples.

When you spell words al-ways no-tice where the ac-cent is re-quir-ed to be pla-ced, and put it on for-ci-bly. And when your teach-er gives out the words of your les-son, lis-ten for the ac-cent-ed syl-la-ble; spell the word, and then pro-nounce it your-self. Thus you will learn by the ear the cor-rect pro-nun-ci-a-tion of words. *Nev-er al-low your-self to pro-nounce a word in-cor-rect-ly.*

LESSON XXXIII.

KINDNESS.

A lit-tle spring had lost its way
A-mid the grass and fern;
A pas-sing stran-ger scoop'd a well
Where wea-ry men might turn;
He wall-ed it in, and hung with care,
A la-dle at the brink.

He thought not of the deed he did,
But wish-ed that men might drink;
He pass-ed again, and lo! the well,
By sum-mers nev-er dried,
Had cool'd ten thou-sand parch-ed tongues,
And sav-ed a life be-side!

SPELLING is an im-por-tant part of ed-u-ca-tion. Boys and girls should learn to spell cor-rect-ly while they are young. If they do not learn it then, they nev-er will. Some per-sons spell ver-y bad-ly. All their friends laugh at them, or pi-ty them. Let it not be so with any of the child-ren of this school. Be-gin at once, and in earn-est. Stud-y close-ly. No-tice ev-e-ry let-ter. Spell each word first *on* the book, and then *off* the book. Make it a point to spell some-thing ev-e-ry day, dur-ing the whole course of your ed-u-ca-tion.

boasts	chants	douse	bumps	bridge
coasts	grants	house	clumps	midge
roasts	plants	louse	dumps	ridge
toasts	slants	mouse	humps	singe
deals	fields	grouse	lumps	cringe
heals	wields	crank	mumps	rinse
meals	yields	drank	pumps	since
peals	beams	flank	rumps	clung
seals	creams	prank	ounce	flung
veals	dreams	blank	pounce	stung

PROVERBS.

A burden one chooses is not felt.
A hasty man never wants woe.
A man is a lion in his own cause.
As you make your bed, so you lie.
Better to be alone than in bad company.
Friendship cannot stand all on one side.
He that would eat the kernel must crack the nut.

LESSON XXXIV.

THE LITTLE DOG.

I like to see a lit-tle dog,
And pat him on the head,
So pret-ti-ly he wags his tail,
When-ev-er he is fed.

Some lit-tle dogs are ver-y good,
And ver-y use-ful too;
And do you know that they will mind
What they are bid to do?

Then I will nev-er beat my dog,
And nev-er give him pain;
Poor fel-low! I will give him food,
And he will love me then.

SPELLING AND DEFINING.

Note.—The exercises in this department are inserted rather as *specimens*, not as parts even of a regular system—our space not permitting the insertion of many examples. But we commend strongly to all teachers the practice of defining some word, term or phrase in every lesson.

a bide	dwell	ab er rant	wan der ing
a bode	dwelt	ab bre vi ate	shor ten
ab duce	with draw	a bil i ty	pow er
ab hor	hate	a bol ish	de stroy
ab ject	mean	ab o li tion	de struc tion
ab rade	rub-off	a bom in ate	ab hor
a bridge	shor ten	a bor tive	fruit less
ab rupt	crag gy	a bridge ment	con trac tion
ab stain	for bear	ab ro gate	re peal
ab sterge	cleanse	ab so lute	com plete
ab stract	sep a rate	ab so lu tion	ac quit tal
ab struse	hid den	ab ster gent	clean ing
a buse	re vile	ac ci dence	gram mar
a byss	gulf	ac com plice	as so ci ate
ac cede	come	ac com plish	ful fil
ac cept	re ceive	ac cre tive	grow ing
ac cess	ap proach	ac cu ra cy	ex act ness
ac cuse	blame	a cer bi ty	sour ness
ac curse	doom	a cute ness	sharp ness
ac quire	gain	ac ri tude	sharp ness
a cute	sharp	ad he rence	at tach ment
ad apt	suit	ad ja cent	con tig u ous
ac quit	free	ad um brate	fore shad ow
ad age	pro verb	ad orn ment	or na ment

If we scrutinize the lives of men of genius, we shall find that activity and persistence are their leading characteristics. Obstacles cannot intimidate, nor labor weary, nor drudgery disgust them.

LESSON XXXV.

DOMESTIC LOVE.

Birds in their little nests agree,
   And 'tis a shameful sight,
When children of one family
   Fall out, and chide, and fight.

Hard names at first, and threat'ning words
   Which are but noisy breath,
May change to clubs and naked swords,
   To murder and to death.

The devil tempts one mother's son
   To rage against another;
So wicked Cain was hurried on,
   Till he had killed his brother.

Pardon, O Lord! our childish rage,
   Our little brawls remove,
That as we grow to riper age,
   Our hearts may all be love.

Words of Two Syllables Accented on the First.

coun ter	con stant	crack er	crotch et
couch ant	con sul	cra dle	crus ty
coun sel	con test	cran kle	cryp tic
count ess	con text	cran ny	crys tal
coun ty	con trite	cra ven	cu bit
coup let	con vent	cray on	cud dle
cour age	con vex	cre dent	cud gel
cour ser	cool er	crea ture	cut ter
cour tier	coop er	cred it	cul prit
court ly	cop per	creep er	cul ture
court ship	co ping	crest ed	cum brous
cous in	cor dage	crev ice	cu rate
cov er	cor ner	crib bage	cur dle

B*

cov ert	cos tal	crick et	cur tain
cov et	cos tive	crim ple	cush ion
cov ey	cost ly	crim son	cut lass
cow ard	cos tume	cri sis	cut throat
coy ly	cot tage	crisp ness	cyg net
coy ness	cot ton	crit ic	cyn ic
coz en	coun cil	cro cus	cym bal

PROFANITY.

The profane abuse of the adorable name of the great Jehovah, before whom all Heaven bows in profoundest reverence, has become shamefully and lamentably prevalent. It is a high criminality. The great God has, by express command, forbidden it, saying: "Thou shalt not take the name of the Lord thy God in vain; for the Lord will not hold him guiltless that taketh his name in vain."

Let every youth be on his guard in relation to this sin. It is evil and only evil continually. And a most fearful account must be rendered for it at the last day. "*Swear not,*" said the Divine Instructor.

LESSON XXXVI.

THE HONEST BOY.

Once there was a little boy,
With curly hair and pleasant eye,
A boy who always told the truth,
And never, never told a lie.

And when he trotted off to school
The children all about would cry,
"There goes the curly headed boy—
The boy that never told a lie."

And every body loved him so,
Because he always told the truth,
That every day, as he grew up,
'Twas said, "There goes the honest youth."

And when the people that stood near
Would turn to ask the reason why,
The answer would be always this,
"Because he never tells a lie."

brinks	crests	worst	didst	slept	beeves
drinks	quests	curst	midst	crept	leaves
links	chests	durst	blest	swept	cleaves
minks	breasts	thirst	chest	grows	splice
pinks	charts	crest	crust	knows	slice
sinks	smarts	guest	trust	doves	trice
winks	first	birth	brunt	loves	saint
clinks	burst	mirth	grunt	shoves	taint
paint	stakes	cringe	sleight	burns	camps
quaint	quakes	fringe	flight	churns	damps
brains	ledge	hinge	plight	spurns	lamps
grains	hedge	singe	slight	turns	clamps
blains	dredge	colts	bright	dines	stamps
chains	pledge	dolts	fright	fines	vamps
drakes	sledge	motes	might	shines	ramps
flakes	wedge	quotes	light	spines	tramps

MONTHS, DAYS AND SEASONS.

The twelve months of the year are divided into four seasons: Spring, Summer, Autumn and Winter. Spring includes March, April and May. The Summer months are June, July and August. The Autumn or Fall season embraces September, October and November. The Winter months are December, January and February.

The number of days belonging to the months respectively is as follows:

> Thirty days have September,
> April, June and November;
> February has twenty-eight alone,
> And all the rest have thirty-one.

LESSON XXXVII.

THE EARTH.

The Earth is a large globe. It is round like a ball. The distance through it is nearly eight thousand miles. It turns around upon its axis once in twenty-four hours. It receives light and heat from the sun.

Darkness is simply the absence of light. That half of the earth which is turned toward the sun has day. That which is turned from it has night.

Although the earth is nearly round, its surface is quite irregular. It has its lofty mountains, and its deep valleys, its hills and its dales, its deserts and its grassy plains, its mighty oceans, and its many streams of water.

It is very pleasing and instructive to read about the different parts of the earth. Every child should strive to obtain that kind of knowledge. The science which treats of the earth's surface is called Geography. It is a very pleasant and useful study.

The science which tells about those parts of the earth which are below the surface is called Geology. It brings to light a great many very curious things. Metals and many other useful things are dug out of the earth.

Words of Two Syllables, Accented on the Second.

ad mit	an nex	at test	com mit
ad vert	an nul	at tent	com press
ad ept	as sert	at tinge	con cern
ad just	at tend	at tune	con fer
at tach	oc cur	ar ray	con fect
ar rest	ob ject	ac cord	con firm
at tract	oc cult	ac cost	con nect
as sent	re dress	ap peal	con sent
de tect	re gard	ap pear	con tent
di rect	re gret	be get	cor rupt
de bar	re ject	be gin	con vict
de test	de ter	be set	con vince
de duct	de fer	de bark	con sist
de mur	re fund	de fect	con sult

LESSON XXXVIII.

JOY AND GRATITUDE.

How thankful should we always be
  That we have life and food;
So little suffering see,
  So much abounding good!

Thus warblers in the wood
  Their cheerful notes employ;
When they've enough of food,
  How constant is their joy!

Then we, with reason's gift,
  And all God's goodness crowned,
Should thus our voices lift,
  And His high praise resound.

The following Words have Opposite Meanings.

free dom	slave ry	in hale	ex hale	hil ly	lev el
feel ing	numb ness	af firm	de ny	dou ble	sin gle
im port	ex port	sim ple	com plex	wis dom	fol ly
col lect	scat ter	a base	ex alt	for mer	lat ter
flour ish	with er	di verge	con verge	lar ger	small er
ma jor	min or	ze nith	na dir	con vex	con cave
small er	great er	sum mer	win ter	cre ate	de stroy
of ten	sel dom	long er	short er	dam age	pro fit
in let	out let	dis sent	a gree	pro fane	sa cred
has ten	loi ter	in duce	e duce	en camp	de camp
for mer	lat ter	in spire	ex pire	ad vance	re treat
i dle	bu sy	pub lic	pri vate	up per	un der
ac tive	clum sy	pret ty	ug ly	in most	out most
mat ter	spir it	in crease	de crease	a bove	be low
love ly	hate ful	pro fuse	stin gy	be hind	be fore
ho ly	sin ful	pa tient	fret ful	ac cept	re ject

A good name is rather to be chosen than great riches; and loving favor rather than silver and gold.

The memory of the just is blessed; but the name of the wicked shall rot.

The righteous shall be had in everlasting remembrance.

He shall be like a tree planted by the rivers of water; his leaf shall not wither.

The ungodly are not so; but are as the chaff which the wind driveth away.—*Bible.*

LESSON XXXIX.
LITTLE THINGS.

Little drops of water,
  Little grains of sand,
Make the mighty ocean
  And the beauteous land.

And the little moments,
  Humble tho' they be,
Make the mighty ages
  Of eternity.

So our little errors
  Lead the soul away
From the paths of virtue,
  Oft in sin to stray.

Little deeds of kindness,
  Little deeds of love,
Make our earth an Eden,
  Like the Heaven above.

Little seeds of mercy,
  Sown by youthful hands,
Grow to bless the nations,
  Far in heathen lands.

Words of Two Syllables, Accented on the Second.

de fine	e lect	ex ceed	ex treme
de grade	em bale	ex claim	ex trude
de lude	em balm	ex clude	ex ude
de gree	em blaze	ex cel	ex ult
de note	em boss	ex cept	for bid
de nude	en chain	ex cern	for get
de pute	en chant	ex cess	ful fil
de range	en close	ex change	gre nade
de duce	en croach	ex cise	hu mane

de rive	en gage	ex cite	il lude
de vote	en large	ex cuse	im mure
dis dain	en joy	ex cuss	im pose
dis course	en list	ex empt	im pure
dis creet	en rich	ex ert	nar rate
dis gust	en robe	ex hale	neg lect
dis join	en rol	ex hort	o pine
dis mount	en snare	ex pand	o mit
dis play	en throne	ex panse	op pose
dis please	en tice	ex pend	ob struct
dis plode	en tire	ex pense	ob ject
dis port	es cort	ex pert	o vert
dis pose	es tate	ex pire	ob tain
dis praise	es teem	ex plain	per tain
dis proof	es trange	ex plode	pre pare
dis prove	e vade	ex plore	pro pose
dis tract	e vent	ex port	re tain
dis tress	e vert	ex pose	re veal
dis turb	e vict	ex press	re vere
e clipse	e vince	ex tant	re voke
e duce	e volve	ex tend	re view
ef fect	ex act	ex tinct	re vise
e lapse	ex alt	ex tort	se crete

PROVERBS.

Reckless youth brings rueful age.
Rule the appetite and temper the tongue.
Ruin is easier made than mended.
Silks and satins put out the kitchen fire.
Search others for virtues, thyself for faults.
Sauce for the goose is sauce for the gander.
Seek a beggar and catch a louse.
Saying and doing are two things.
Send a thief to catch a thief.
Sharp appetites need no rich sauces.
She shows more airs than graces.

LESSON XL.
LOVE ONE ANOTHER.

A little girl with happy look,
Sat slowly reading a pond'rous book,
All bound with velvet and edged with gold,
And its weight was more than the child could hold;
And dearly she loved to ponder it o'er,
And every day she prized it more,
For, as she looked at her dear little brother,
It said, "Little children must love one another."

She thought it was beautiful in that book,
And the lesson home to her heart she took;
She walked on her way with a trusting grace
And a dove-like look on her meek young face,
Which said as plain as words could say,
The Holy Bible I must obey;
So, mamma, I'll be kind to my darling brother.

I am sorry he is naughty and will not pray,
But I'll love him still, for I think the way
To make him kind and gentle to me,
Will be better shown, if I let him see
I strive to do what I think is right;
And thus when I kneel to pray to-night,
I will clasp my arms around my brother,
And say, "Little children must love one another."

The little girl did as the Bible taught,
And pleasant indeed was the change it wrought;
For the boy looked up in glad surprise,
To meet the light of her loving eyes;
His heart was full, he could not speak,
He pressed a kiss on his sister's cheek;
And God looked down on the happy mother,
Whose little children loved each other.

clams	words	blains	brawls	batch
drams	works	chains	crawls	catch
crams	worms	scrapes	shawls	hatch
skims	bunch	drapes	sprawls	latch
swims	lunch	grapes	yawls	match
plums	munch	crones	brash	snatch

drums	bones	drones	crash	swamp
scraps	cones	jerks	march	swarm
straps	stones	smerks	starch	drawn
barks	blinds	shells	parch	spawn
marks	minds	smells	squash	lawns
sparks	winds	swells	swash	yawns

A RUINED CHARACTER.

The poet's assertion that "the boy is father to the man"—that is, shapes his destiny, is strikingly illustrated by the following incidents:

Not long since, in a certain neighborhood, a man was wandering in search of employment. He called at a respectable farmer's house, and told his errand.

"What is your name?" asked the man.

"Jonathan Gilman," was the reply.

"Jonathan Gilman! the same who lived near here when a boy?"

"The same, sir."

"I will not employ you then."

Poor Jonathan, surprised at such a reply, passed on to the next farmer's; but the same reply was given. He soon came in sight of an old school-house.

"Ah," said he, "I understand it now. I was a school boy there once, but what kind of school boy? Lazy and disobedient. And although I am now in a measure reformed, they all think me the same kind of a man as I was a boy. O that I had done my duty when at school! then again could I dwell pleasantly in the land of of my birth."

School boys and school girls, please remember that your school mates will be likely to look upon you in manhood or womanhood as they did in youth. Then, in your school days, prepare for noble men and women.

LESSON XLI.

PROVERBS.

A lie has no legs, but scandal has wings.
A bad workman quarrels with his tools.
A happy heart makes a blooming countenance.
A clear conscience fears no accusation.
A fat kitchen makes a lean will.

A fault confessed is half redressed.
A fool and his money are soon parted.
A chip of the old block. After death the doctor.
A friend in need is a friend indeed.
A good name keeps its lustre in the dark.
A good word is as soon said as an ill one.
Where the miser has trod the goose cannot graze.
A great dowry is a bed full of troubles.
A light heeled mother—a heavy heeled daughter.
All are not hunters that blow the horn.
All is not gold that shines.

Words so nearly alike that they may be used for each other.

art ful	craf ty	cun ning	re nounce
bos ky	syl van	ru ral	dis own
bon ny	hand some	pret ty	back bite
clam my	vis cus	sli my	de fame
dis mal	lu rid	gloom y	de prave
ea ger	ar dent	ear nest	cor rupt
es say	at tempt	tri al	ex hort
be hest	com mand	man date	ad vise
das tard	cow ard	pol troon	ex pand
as sault	at tack	on set	ex tend
ad age	prov erb	say ing	im pede
bib ber	tip pler	drunk ard	re tard
bod y	sub stance	mat ter	se date
af fairs	con cerns	bu si ness	so ber
ail ment	ill ness	sick ness	in tend
pu pil	stu dent	schol ar	de sign
ten or	pur port	mean ing	dan dle
rap ine	plun der	pil lage	ca ress
vor tex	ed dy	whirl pool	ig nite
res ponse	re ply	an swer	in flame
hear say	ru mor	re port	reck on
bol ster	cush ion	pil low	com pute
gar bage	of fal	ref use	con sole
cus tom	prac tice	u sage	com fort
gen tile	hea then	Pa gan	bur nish
for ceps	pin cers	nip pers	pol ish
thral dom	slave ry	bon dage	pre dict
reck on	com pute	num ber	fore tell

CHINESE WALL.

This famous structure is one of the most remarkable monuments of human industry on the face of the globe. It passes over high mountains, and crosses deep valleys. In many places it is strongly built, and fortified with towers, at regular intervals. It is, for the most part, of brick, resting on foundations of stone. It is twelve hundred and fifty miles long, and it employed several millions of men five years in its construction.

LESSON XLII.

HOME AND FRIENDS.

Oh, there's a power to make each hour
  As sweet as heaven designed it;
Nor need we roam to bring it home,
  Though few there be who find it!

We seek too high for things close by,
  And lose what nature found us;
For life has here no charms so dear
  As Home and Friends around us!

We oft destroy the present joy
  For future hopes—and praise them;
While flowers as sweet bloom at our feet
  If we'd but stoop to raise them!

For things afar still sweetest are,
  When youth's bright spell hath bound us;
But soon we're taught that earth hath naught
  Like Home and Friends around us!

The Friends that speed in time of need,
  When Hope's last reed is shaken,
To show us still, that come what will,
  We are not quite forsaken!

Though all were night—if but the light
  From Friendship's altar crown'd us,
'Twould prove the bliss of earth was this—
  Our Home and Friends around us!

PROVERBS.

He that lives badly one year sorrows for it seven.
He that reckons without his host may reckon again.
He that runs fast will not run long.
He that runs in the night stumbles.
He that stays in the valley will never get over the hill.
He who sows not corn plants thistles.
He that will not be counselled cannot be helped.
He that will steal an egg will steal an ox.
He that rises late, never does a good day's work.
He that runs after a shadow has a wearisome race.
He that sows brambles must not go bare foot.
He who swims in sin will sink in sorrow.
He who would catch fish must not mind getting wet.
Hiders are good finders. Hot sup, hot swallow.
Home is home, be it ever so homely.
Humility is the foundation of all virtue.
I can see as far into a mill stone as the picker.
Idle folks have the most labor.
If the cap fits, wear it. Kissing goes by favor.
Idleness is the parent of want and shame.

Words of Three Syllables, Accented on the First.

ab ne gate	ac tu al	come li ness
ab ro gate	an i mal	com for ter
ab so lute	an i mate	com ic al
ab so nant	an nal ist	com mi grate
ab sti nence	an nu al	com pe tent
ab la tive	an nu lar	com mo dore
ac o lent	an nu let	com mon er
ad di ble	an o dyne	cor mo rant
am e thyst	an o my	com plais ance
am i ty	an swer er	com pli ment
am o rist	an te date	com pli cate
am o rous	an te lope	com pro mise
am ple ness	an te past	con di ment
am pli ate	choc o late	con fi dent
am pli fy	cic a trice	con fi dence
am pli tude	cic a trize	con flu ent

am pu tate	cal cu late	but ter fly
am u let	cim e ter	cab i net
an a gram	cir cu lar	cal e fy
an a lyze	cir cu late	cal i ber
an a pest	cir cum flex	cal o mel
am bas sage	cit i zen	cal um ny
am bi ent	civ il ize	cap ti vate
am i ty	clar i on	cas u ist
am nes ty	clar i fy	cat a combs
an ces tor	cal an der	car ni val
an ces try	col li quate	car a van
and i ron	col lo cate	ca pa ble
an ec dote	col lo quy	cat a ract
an ge lot	col o nize	cat a pult
an gli can	col o ny	cen tu ry
an gri ly	col or ing	cen' tri cal
an gu lar	col or less	cir cu lar
an gu lous	com bat ant	cen ti pede
an cho vy	com bi nate	cen tu ple
ap er ture	com e dy	cer ti fy

LESSON XLIII.

AGAINST IDLENESS.

How doth the little busy bee
   Improve each shining hour,
And gather honey all the day,
   From every opening flower.

How skillfully she builds her cell,
   How neat she spreads her wax!
And labors hard to store it well,
   With the sweet food she makes.

In works of labor, or of skill,
   I should be busy too;
For Satan finds some mischief still,
   For idle hands to do.

In books, or work, or healthful play,
   Let my first years be past,
That I may give, for every day,
   Some good account at last.

Words of Two Syllables, Accented on the First.

mar ble	mind ful	num ber	pil grim
mar gin	mod est	nurs ling	pin cers
mar ket	mon ster	nov ice	pig my
mar mot	mys tic	new ly	pis tol
mar tin	mil ler	nim ble	priv et
mar quis	mil ky	nine ty	priv y
mar vel	min im	Nes tor	pub lish
mas tiff	muf fler	op tic—	pun ish
mem ber	mum ble	oc tave	pun ster
mus lin	muz zle	or gan	pur ple
mus ter	mur mur	om let	print er
mer cer	mus ty	ot ter	pur chase
mit tens	mut ton	pen cil	
mir ror	mum my	pen ny	

PROVERBS.

Good works cost nothing; but are of great value.
Have not the cloak to make when it begins to rain.
If you wish a thing done, go; if not, send.
Men apt to promise are apt to forget.
In a calm sea every man is pilot.
Alms-giving never made any man poor, nor robbery rich, nor prosperity wise.
A liar is not believed when he speaks the truth.
Forget others' faults by remembering your own.
It costs more to revenge injuries than to bear them.
Never be weary of well-doing.
One ill example spoils many good precepts.

LESSON XLIV.

WORKS AND POWER OF GOD.

There's not a plant or flower below
   But makes God's glories known;
And clouds arise and tempests blow,
   By order from His throne.

Creatures, as numerous as they be,
  Are subject to his care;
There's not a place where we can flee,
  But God is present there.

His hand is my perpetual guard,
  He keeps me with His eye;
Why should I forget the Lord,
  Who is forever nigh?

The good Samaritan occupies a high niche in the temple of fame; but the cold hearted wretches who despised the sufferings of him that was ready to perish are consigned to everlasting infamy.

To do good, and to communicate, forget not; for with such sacrifices God is well pleased.

Words of Three Syllables, Accented on the Second.

a base ment	con clu sive	in de cent
a tone ment	de lu sive	ad ja cent
a bu sive	en case ment	e lope ment
ad he sive	en tail ment	en du rance
ac cu ser	en rol ment	en snare ment
ar ri val	in cite ment	en fee ble
de base ment	in ci sor	e qua tor
de ci sive	in ci sive	e rase ment
cor ro sive	in he sive	hi a tus
he ro ic	nar ra tor	di vi sor
hu mane ly	cu ra tor	Pa go da
de mure ly	en no ble	ad ju tor
se cure ly	en a ble	Oc to ber
sin cere ly	ob scure ly	de port ment
sur vey or	se rene ly	de po nent
pur vey or	se date ness	po ma tum
sur vey ing	en slave ment	po ta to
de fray ment	dis fa vor	de ba tor

nar ra tor	tor pe do	un sta ble	
ac cu ser	tor na do	un seem ly	
re fu sal	in tru der	ac quaint ance	
de tru sive	vi ra go	ac quire ment	
a muse ment	pro fuse ly	a bode ment	
en su rer	ver bose ly	ar thrit ic	
su pine ly	se date ly	as bes tos	
su preme ly	se date ness	at ten tive	
un time ly	mo rose ness	at tor ney	
en tire ly	un sha ken	a ver ment	

LESSON XLV.

SOURCES OF LIGHT.

The moon and planets, while they run,
    Their circles round the night,
Receive their lustre from the sun,
    Source of created light.

Angels and saints on earth alone
    Beauty and bliss obtain,
From Him that sits upon the throne,
    The Lamb, that once was slain.

Oh sun of righteousness, impart
    Thy glorious light divine;
On every school, in every heart,
    Arise and ever shine.

Words of Two Syllables, Accented on the First.

ran ter	shut ter	stub born	tur nip
ren der	shuf fle	stur dy	ty rant
ros in	sim per	sub ject	twen ty
rot ten	sin gle	sul len	twist ed
rec tor	sick ness	sum mon	var nish
rus ty	sim ple	sur face	vap id
seg ment	sys tem	sur plus	ver min
sev er	skill ful	swel try	ver dure

sex ton	skit tish	tar dy	vis age
sen try	six ty	tat ter	vig ils
ser pent	squan der	tax es	vict uals
six pence	squal id	tap ster	vi ands
shel ter	stam mer	tor rid	vic tim
shiv er	stin gy	tur gid	vil lain

THE LOSS OF EARLY PURITY OF CHARACTER.

Over the beauty of the plum and the apricot, there grows a bloom and beauty more exquisite than the fruit itself—a soft delicate plush that overspreads its blushing cheek. Now if you strike your hand over that, and it is once gone, it is gone forever, for it never grows but once.

Take the flower that hangs in the morning impearled in dew—arrayed as no queenly woman ever was arrayed with jewels. Once shake it so that the beads roll off, and you may sprinkle water over it as carefully as you please, yet it can never be made again what it was when the dew fell silently upon it from heaven! On a frosty morning you may see the panes of glass covered with landscape, mountains, lakes, trees, blending in a beautiful, fantastic picture. Now lay your hand upon the glass, and by the scratch of your finger, or by the warmth of your palm, all the delicate tracery will be obliterated.

So there is in youth a beauty and purity of character, which when once touched and defiled, can never be restored; a fringe more delicate than frost work, and which, when torn or broken, will never be re-embroidered. A man who has spotted and spoiled his garments in youth, though he may seek to make them white again, can never wholly do it, even were he to wash them with his tears.

When a young man leaves his father's house, with the blessings of his mother's tears still wet upon his forehead, if he once loses that early purity of character, it is a loss that he never can make whole again. Such is the consequence of crime. Its effects cannot be eradicated; it can only be forgiven. It is a stain of blood that we can never make white, and which can be washed away only in the blood of Christ that "cleanseth from all sin!"

C

LESSON XLVI.

THE BIRD OF SPRING.

Sweet bird, thy bower is ever fair,
Thy sky is ever clear;
Thou hast no sorrow in thy song,
No winter in thy year.

EMPHASIS.

That force of utterance which we give to certain words, to bring out their sense strongly, is called *emphasis*. It is very important, both in speaking and reading, to consider what the *sense* requires, and so to place the *emphasis* as to bring it fully out. Below you will find several examples for frequent practice. Your teachers will take pleasure also in furnishing many more: Be *studious*, and you will *excel*. It is easier to *lose* than to *gain*. Those who *swell* in *prosperity* will *shrink* in *adversity*. When *man* sins *angels* weep and *devils* rejoice. We live in *two* worlds—a *natural* and a *spiritual* world. Science has no *enemy*, except *ignorance*. We cannot *love* those whom we do not *respect*. The *good* man has God in his *heart*, even when He is not in his *mouth;* but the *hypocrite* has God in his *mouth* without having Him in his *heart*. Nothing *sow*, nothing *reap*.

Words of Two Syllables, Accented on the First.

bab ble	pop lar	beg gar	kin dle
gan der	gen der	sud den	lim ber
hin der	gip sy	pot ter	cam el
gen tile	pul ley	gird er	gar ment
bun dle	gar ret	gel id	pon der
glib ly	plun der	rav age	pim ple
lob ster	bal lad	glim mer	ger man
ges ture	pad dle	suck er	sul len
mid dle	glean er	buf fet	gar net
gin gle	spat ter	gar nish	glo ry
mar mot	mag pie	prim er	cam let
glow worm	glow ing	ket tle	pud dle

gen try	pot ter	glov er	glu ten
suf fer	gir dle	pip pin	gar land
gath er	gaunt let	girl ish	rav age
hud dle	*h*um ble	gloom y	rab ble
sim ple	sin gle	lum ber	gar lick
gleam y	glee ful	ger und	g*h*ast ly
trav el	dam son	geor gic	sim mer
glis ten	glit ter	rad dish	scat ter
grav el	bit ter	glob ule	mat ter
if fin	pil grim	buc kle	mar vel

IMPORTANT TRUTHS.

It signifies nothing to say we will not change our religion, if our religion does not change us.

A desire for happiness is *natural*; a desire after holiness is supernatural.

If you forget God when you are young, God will forget you when you are old.

LESSON XLVII.

THE SUN.

MORAL DUTIES.

My God, who makes the sun to know
   His proper hour to rise,
And give light to all below,
   Doth send him round the skies.

When from the chambers of the east
   His morning race begins,
He never tires nor stops to rest,
   But round the world he shines.

So, like the sun, would I fulfill
   The business of the day;
Begin my work betimes, and still
   March on my heavenly way.

Give me, O Lord, thy early grace,
   Nor let my soul complain,
That the young morning of my days
   Has all been spent in vain.

THE SHIP.

How gloriously her gallant course she goes!
Her white wings flying—never from her foes;
She walks the waters like a thing of life,
And seems to dare the elements to strife.
Who would not brave the battle-fire—the wreck—
To move the monarch of her peopled deck?

Words of Four Syllables, Accented on the Second.

a cad e mist	anx i e ty	cir cum fer en cords
a cad e my	a pol o gy	cli mac ter ic
ac cel er ate	a pol o gist	co ad ju tor
ac cen tu ate	a pol o gize	co er ci ble
ac com mo date	ap pel la tive	co hab i tant
ac com pa ny	ap prov a ble	co in ci dence
ac cos ta ble	col le gi ate	con com i tant
ac coun ta ble	col le gi an	col lec tive ly
ac cou tre ment	e mer gen cy	col lo qui al
ac cred it ed	em phat i cal	com mem o rate
ac cus tom ance	em pov er ish	com men da ble
ad dec i mate	en cour age ment	com mo di ous
a men i ty	en tab la ture	com mod i ty
am phib i ous	en ta ble ment	com mu ni cate
am phib o lous	ex ter mi nate	com par i son
am plif i cate	ex tem por ize	com pen sa tive
a myg da late	ca cu mi nate	com pen sa ble
a nal o gous	cal ca ri ous	com pla cen cy
a nal o gy	ca lig i nous	con cat e nate
a nal y sis	ca lid i ty	con ceiv a ble
a naph o ra	ca mel o pard	con cil i ate
a nas tro phe	ca non i cal	con fis ca ble
a nath e ma	can thar i des	con form a ble
a nat o mize	ca pac i tate	con form i ty
an drog i nal	ca pac i ty	con glom er ate
an droph a gus	ca par i son	con glu ti nate
a nem os cope	ca pit u late	con serv a tive
an gel i cal	cap tiv i ty	con serv a tor
a nil i ty	car nal i ty	con sid er ate

an nu i tant   car nos i ty   con sist ent ly
an nu i ty   car niv o rous   con sis to ry
an tip a thy   ca thol i cism   con sol i date
an tis tro phe   con tes i mal   con ven ti cle

LESSON XLVIII.

INNOCENCE.

THE TURTLE DOVE.

When good Nathaniel's praise I read,
  In Scripture page renown'd;
"Behold an Israelite indeed,
  In whom no guile is found;"

His fame, I'm sure is higher far
  Than kings or heroes gain,
Who reap their laurels in the war,
  But not without a stain.

The gentle words that banish strife,
  Our common joys increase;
But what is home, and what is life,
  Without the bond of peace!

Then would'st thou earn thy Savior's praise,
  Whose eye regards the young,
Let meek discretion guide thy ways,
  And kindness rule thy tongue.

So shalt thou learn to keep in sight
  The wisdom from above,
And with it always to unite
  The mildness of the dove.

Spelling and Defining.

al ti tude   height   eu cha rist   sac ra ment
ar mis tice   truce   u ni ty   one ness
ar ti fice   de vice   ev it ate   a void
dom i cil   house   ag it ate   shake
ve hi cle   car ri age ex e crate   curse
sur cin gle   girth   ex e cute   fin ish

rem e dy	cure	dis cre pance	dif fer ence
res i due	re main der	fu mi gate	smoke
cav i ty	hol low	ev i dence	proof
fo li age	leaves	es ti mate	val ue
cra ni um	skull	ex er cise	ex ert
con di ment	sauce	fam i ly	house hold
can ti cle	song	dis pu tant	rea son er
or i son	pray er	di a dem	crown
lon gi tude	length	di a phragm	mid riff
syl lo gism	ar gu ment	dul ci fy	sweet en
sym me try	beau ty	dul co rate	sweet en
com pro mit	pledge	ful mi nate	thun der
dig ni ty	gran deur	in du rate	har den
di a lect	speech	ir ri gate	wa ter
id i ot	fool	el e vate	raise
in te ger	whole	sig ni fy	mean
de vi ous	rov ing	tu me fy	swell
fir ma ment	sky	fab ri cate	frame
des ti ny	fate	im i tate	re sem ble
dis si pate	scat ter	oc cu py	hold
dif fer ent	un like	cu mu late	heap
dif fi cult	hard	hes i tate	stop
dig ni fy	ad vance	com pli cate	en tan gle

ANECDOTE.

A conceited magistrate was driving a pair of unruly oxen. Finding that they had no reverence for his authority, he leaped from his cart, took each by the horns, shook them severely, and exclaimed: Why don't you obey the Magistrate as the Scriptures direct, especially as I have more sense than both of you put together?

LESSON XLIX.

WHO MADE THE WORLD?

'Twas *God* that formed the concave sky,
And all the shining orbs on high,
Who gave the various beings birth,
That peopled all the spacious earth.

'Tis HE that bids the tempests rise,
And rolls the thunder thro' the skies;
His voice the elements obey,
Through all the earth extends his sway.

His goodness all His creatures share,
But *man* is His peculiar care;
Then while they all proclaim His praise,
Let *man* his voice the loudest raise.

THE SUN.

The Sun is a body of immense size. Thirteen hundred thousand globes, as large as our earth, might be formed from it. Its distance is ninety-five millions of miles from the earth. It is the great source of *light* and *heat*, not only to our globe, but to the entire solar system.

The word "system" means *placed together*. As the head, the chest, and the several other members of our bodies make up the *human* system, so the solar system consists of the sun and the planets which revolve round it. It is called the *solar* system from the Latin word "Sol," the name given to the sun in that language.

The sun is the centre of that system. All the planets revolve round it at different distances. The attraction of that immense body—the sun—holds them all in their places.

Take a small weighty body, tie a string to it and then throw it round your hand in a circle. The body will represent a planet. The string will represent the sun's attraction. The force which you give it causes it to go forward; but going forward, and yet held to the centre by the attracting force, it must move in a circle.

Now take a slate, make a small central figure on it for the sun. Then draw eight circles around it—the first one very near to the sun, each one outside being more distant.

Place on those circles the eight first letters of the alphabet, putting A on the one nearest the sun, and you will have a correct idea of the solar system.

The circles in which the planets move are called their *orbits*. The sun being the centre, does not revolve in a circle like the planets; but it turns round, like a grindstone, upon its own axis, once in twenty-five days.

QUESTIONS.

What is the sun? Its size? Distance? Of what is it the source? Meaning of the word *system*? Of what does the solar system consist? Why called *solar*? What is the centre of the system? What revolve round it? How describe that system? What holds the planets together? How many principal planets? What are those circles called? Does the sun revolve in a circle? In what time does it turn upon its axis?

LESSON L.

GOD'S CARE AND LOVE.

There's not a plant, or blooming flower,
In field or fragrant bower;
But shows the constant care and love
Of God who reigns above.

BOTANY.

This science gives a sort of natural history of the vegetable kingdom. Trees, shrubs, plants, grasses, mosses, flowers, fruits—all these come under review.

The different modes of arranging this great kingdom into classes afford high gratification to persons of enquiring minds.

Little folks are commonly delighted with the examination of the several parts of the flowers, of different plants. They are wonderful structures. Not only are they very beautiful, but they are very useful. Without flowers there would be no seeds, no grains, no fruits.

This science displays many wonders. The study of it improves, delights and refines the mind. Young people should all study it. Our climate is very favorable for it. The South also abounds in rich specimens of great variety. The *evergreens*, especially, are very numerous.

Words of Two Syllables, Accented on the Second.

ad mire	re store	de light	ca jole
ad dict	ob scure	di rect	pis tole
de bar	a dore	en list	a tone
de base	en tire	in sist	de note
ca rouse	ex pire	com pute	dis suade
ob tain	en force	se rene	in snare
com plain	em brace	sur mise	se lect
be moan	sus pire	un true	re flect
dis ease	se date	un stop	as sert
de pose	in flate	be wail	a vert
post pone	fo ment	un veil	per vert
sug gest	mo lest	re tail	sus pense
re quest	di gest	vo lute	im pair
fre quent	ex ist	ob serve	im pale
re quire	exempt	ob scene	in scribe
con spire	ex ert	de plore	de tain
ex plore	some times	in case	at tain
ab jure	re quite	ac crue	de pose

LESSON LI.

CALM AND THANKFUL.

Father, whate'er of earthly bliss
   Thy sovereign will denies,
Accepted at Thy throne of grace,
   Let this petition rise.

Give me a calm and thankful heart,
   From every murmur free,
The blessing of Thy grace impart,
   And make me live to Thee.

Let the sweet hope that Thou art mine,
   My life and death attend;
Thy presence thro' my journey shine,
   And crown my journey's end.

C*

ANECDOTES.

The celebrated Doctor Andrew Fuller, in a jocular mood, said one day to his clerical friend, Dr. Sparrowhawk: "Do tell me, Doctor, what difference there is between a Sparrowhawk and an Owl?" "A wide difference," said he. "An owl is *fuller* in the head, *fuller* in the breast, and *fuller* all over."

Dr. Parr, who was regarded as a walking library, in his day, was thus accosted by a conceited Sophomore:— "Doctor, an idea has struck me. Suppose you and I make a *book*." "That is right," said the Doctor. "Let me put into it all that I know, and you put in all that you *do not know*, and we shall make a book that Jonah's whale could not swallow."

Words of Two Syllables, Accented on the First.

fin ish	fur nish	flip pant	for mer
fun nel	fore head	fore most	fop pish
fit ful	flax en	gran ite	grit ty
gaunt let	gal lon	gal lop	gos sip
gos ling	gras sy	grum ble	grant ed
growl er	glow ing	gloom y	heal ing
hast en	hire ling	hope ful	hot spur
home ly	hol ster	jail er	leak y
her ring	hope less	home spun	hind rance
meek ness	mourn ing	mu sic	mea sles
life long	lap wing	lath er	lan tern
nu bile	nee dle	noth ing	ni trous
name less	no dous	neat ness	pat ent
paint er	pal ace	pan tile	pas ture
pre script	plain tiff	pick et	pock et
pom pous	pew ter	pha sis	phan tom
rai ment	rain y	ran cid	read er
rea son	reap er	roll er	row el
sap less	suit or	se rous	si phon
sky light	shoul der	ship ment	sneak ing
sleep er	slut tish	speech less	spon sor
spon dee	spike nard	spot less	spoil er

LESSON LII.

THE ROSE.

MENTAL BEAUTY.

The Rose, the sweetly blooming rose,
    E'er from the tree 'tis torn,
Is like the charm which beauty shows,
    In life's exulting morn.

But oh! how soon its sweets are gone,
    How soon it withering lies;
So when the eve of life comes on,
    Sweet beauty fades and dies.

Then since the fairest form that's made
    Soon withering we shall find,
Let us possess what ne'er can fade,
    The beauties of the mind.

Words of Two Syllables, Accented on the First.

gar den	hunt er	grif fin	lan cet
gar ner	hunts man	glim mer	lem on
gar gle	hur dle	ham mer	les son
gen der	in come	ham let	lim ber
gen tle	in most	hin der	lim pid
gid dy	in cest	hun ter	lim ner
gig gle	in dex	hur ry	lov er
giv er	jar gon	ker sey	low ly
ham per	jest er	kin dred	loy al
hap pen	jus tice	kins man	lum ber
bar per	jum ble	lin den	lus tre
help er	jun to	lis ten	mas ter
hid den	ker nel	liv er	mat ter
hin der	kit ten	liv id	man ly

HOW TO LEARN A LESSON.

An easy lesson may appear,
    At first, too hard for me,
Although to others very clear,
    And simple as can be.

If with good will I try to learn,
  Soon I shall find it plain;
But if in haste I from it turn,
  Hard it will still remain.

It will not do to think or say,
  'Tis of no use to try;
To give it up is not the way,
  Nor yet to fret or cry.

The way to make that lesson plain,
  Which now too hard I find,
Is but to *try*, and *try again*,
  With all my heart and mind.

LESSON LIII.

THE FIRMAMENT OF HIS POWER.

The spacious firmament on high,
With all the blue, ethereal sky,
And spangled Heavens, a shining frame,
Their great Original proclaim.

The unwearied sun, from day to day,
Does his Creator's power display,
And publishes to every land
The work of an Almighty hand.

Soon as the evening shades prevail,
The moon takes up the wondrous tale,
And nightly to the listening earth,
Repeats the story of her birth.

While all the stars that round her burn,
And all the planets in their turn,
Confirm the tidings as they roll,
And spread the truth from pole to pole.

What tho' in solemn silence all
Move round this dark terrestrial ball;
What tho' no real voice nor sound
Amidst those radiant orbs be found?

In reason's ear they all rejoice,
And utter forth a glorious voice;
Forever singing as they shine,
"The hand that made us is divine."
[Addison.

Words of Two Syllables, Accented on the Second.

de bate	con fuse	con sole	ap prize
re late	ob late	im pale	ap proach
cre ate	be rate	nar rate	ap pulse
se date	be late	re tain	ap ply
col late	in flate	re main	a right
pro bate	sur vey	de tain	a rise
con nate	in lay	pro claim	a venge
a base	mis lay	de cry	a wake
de lay	de cay	do main	a ward
a buse	por tray	ob tain	a way
al cade	a stray	ap pease	a woke
ar cade	es teem	ap pear	a wry
pa rade	re deem	ap pend	ba shaw
pre pare	ca reen	ap plaud	be spice
ac cuse	de claim	ap plause	be spread
re fuse	con dole	ap ply	blas pheme
pro fuse	pa role	ap praise	block ade

There is no "card" that so certainly leads to fortune as the "*spade*" when well employed in the field or garden.

A wag, down East, wrote over the door of a schoolhouse: "The New England Whaling Institution."

The poor man who was overwhelmed by astonishment has not yet been dug out.

An Irishman's prescription for making cannon was: 'Take a long *hole* and pour melted brass round it."

LESSON LIV.

WOMAN.

Not she with traitorous kiss the Savior stung,
Not she denied him with unholy tongue;
She, when Apostles shrank, was steadfast, brave,
Last at the cross, and earliest at the grave.

PROVERBS.

A lazy man loves a willing horse.
A little pot is soon hot. All the fat's in the fire.
A man may buy gold too dear.
An honest man's word is as good as his bond.
An idle brain is the devil's work-shop.
An oak is not felled with one blow.
A pitcher often to the well, but broken at last.
A rolling stone gathers no moss.
A quiet conscience sleeps in thunder.
A rotten sheep infects the whole flock.
A single fact outweighs a ship load of theory.
A small pack befits a small peddler.
A spur in the head is worth two in the heel.
A wager is a fool's argument.
A willing mind makes a light foot.
A word before is worth two behind.
Beggars have no right to be choosers.
Be slow to promise, but quick to perform.
Better to round than fall into the ditch.
Better ride an ass that carries than a horse that throws.
Birds of the feather flock together.
Borrowed garments never fit well.

Words of Three Syllables, Accented on the Third.

ad ver tise	su per vise	com mi nute
bar ri cade	un der mine	com pre hend
cir cum vent	un der go	con de scend
cir cum volve	o ver leap	con tra vene
dis es teem	o ver top	coun ter act
dis u nite	ap per tain	coun ter charge
deb o nair	in ter leave	coun ter charm
dom i neer	in ter vene	coun ter mand
dis re pute	un der went	coun ter march
de com pose	un der sell	coun ter mine
dis em bark	o ver hang	coun ter poise
dis ap pear	ap pre hend	coun ter vail
dis in ter	ar e nose	cour te san
dis a gree	auc tion eer	de com pose

in com mode	co in cide	dev o tee
ab sen tee	co a lesce	dis en gage
an te cede	co ag ment	dis em bark
an te pone	co ex ist	dis o bey
con tra vene	col on ade	dis re gard

LESSON LV.

THE CHICKENS.

At night, the chickens sleep under the wings of the old hen. In the morning, they are out very early, and they run about the grounds very actively, picking up seeds, bugs and worms for breakfast. Thomas, looking at them one morning, said to little Mary:

  See, sister, how the chickens trip,
    So busy in the morn ;
  Look how their heads they dip and dip,
    To pick the scattered corn.

  Dear sister, shall we shut our eyes,
    And to the light be blind ;
  Nor think of Him who food supplies
    To us and all mankind ?

  Whether our wants be great or small,
    Or rich or poor our fare,
  To Heaven above, we owe for all,
    The voice of praise and prayer.

Words of Two Syllables, Accented on the Second.

im pute	con tain	en dear
pol lute	em ploy	be deck
de mure	de ploy	be dew
so cure	ad join	be dim
in case	en join	be drench
mis state	re join	be dust
re plete	pur loin	be fall
de plete	de stroy	be fit
com plete	an noy	be fool
trans late	al loy	be fore

se crete	de coy	be foul
ig nite	en joy	be gin
re cite	a void	be gird
po lite	de void	be gone
in cite	de vour	be grim
ar ray	ca rouse	be guile
a way	es pouse	be gun
un say	a mount	be have
dis may	sur mount	be head
o bey	en dow	be held
de ny	a vow	be hest
re ply	al low	be hind
sup ply	re boil	be hold
im ply	tur moil	be·half
com ply	be wray	be hoof
be tray	as tray	be 'lie
af fray	ca reer	be lief

EXERCISE.

Exercise in the open air is essential to health and enjoyment. Without it the body becomes feeble, the countenance pale and dejected, the spirits depressed and gloomy. On the contrary, suitable exercise regularly taken, creates a healthy appetite, invigorates the powers of digestion, produces sound and refreshing sleep, causes freshness of complexion and cheerfulness of spirits, wards off disease, and tends to preserve the vigor of both the body and the mind to an advanced age.

LESSON LVI.

THE WICKED BOY.

Harry Blount had a very kind and good mother. She did all for him that a mother could do, but he was very unkind and wicked. He would do nothing that she wished him to do; but he did all he could to vex her. He would let the hogs into the garden, turn the calves in with the cows, break up the nests of her hens, and cut the bark off her shade trees. He would lie, swear, get drunk, steal, fight, and do everything that was vile.

His mother sent him to school, but he did not like to

go. He would play by the way, or go off into the woods, and stay till the school was out.

But he could not be idle there. He spent his time in killing lizzards, bees, bugs and young birds. To take *life* was his delight. At home it was the same way.

He threw his little sister's pet kitten into the fire and burnt it to death. Her charming little canary bird he fed on poison berries and killed it. He soon became so bad that everybody despised him. So he could not stay at home. At last he ran away. He went to a distant town to get something to do; but his bad name followed him, and no body would employ him. He became a beggar and had to lie out in the streets.

Soon he was caught robbing a store, and was put in jail. There he killed one of his fellow-prisoners. *He was hung as a murderer*—deeply lamenting all his folly and wickedness *when it was too late!*

How true it is that "a bad beginning makes a bad end?" "*Evil slays the wicked.*"

Words of Two Syllables, Accented on the First.

ab bess	ab sence	bar rack	con text
ab scess	an ise	ac cent	ad verse
ar dent	ac tress	ad junct	ag ile
ad dice	am bler	branch y	al ley
am bler	an swer	bas tard	cam let
an swer	an them	blos som	blus ter
cap tor	cap tive	can ker	bant ling
car riage	blan dish	ham mock	cal lous
bap tism	ban quet	can dor	car rot
cul prit	cap tain	com merce	com ic
cas sock	Cash mere	con vert	chat tel
chal ice	clas sic	con vent	cross ness
dac tyl	chal lenge	con vict	com mon
chand ler	chol er	cor ner	cov et
chap lain	chan cre	com ment	cut lass
dan druff	das tard	doc ile	dog ma
dol lar	doc trine	fab ric	dam age
dol phin	dor ick	fam ine	fath om
flac cid	flan nel	fran tic	feath er

AN ATTRACTIVE PICTURE.

There were once three very attractive children, whose names were Gustavus, Herman and Annie. Their father owned a large estate, and they went forth one day to gather flowers in his fields. They were very happy in their sports, because they loved each other, and each strove to increase their mutual enjoyment.

After playing awhile they agreed to separate, and to collect each a bunch of favorite flowers. When this was done, they met again beneath the branches of a noble tree.

"I have chosen the *violet*," said Gustavus, "because it is fragrant and modest." And he gave his violets to Herman and Annie.

Herman said : "I have chosen the *lily*, because it is the emblem of innocence. I love it, because it reminds me of a pure heart and the love of my Father in Heaven." And he gave his beautiful lilies to Gustavus and Annie.

Annie produced a bunch of *forget-me-nots*, and said: "I have chosen the forget-me-not, because it is the flower of love and tenderness." Then Annie gave her forget-me-nots to Gustavus and Herman.

After this, these lovely children agreed to weave their flowers into crowns, which they carried home and placed on the brows of their father and mother. This affectionate conduct delighted their parents ; and thus, by innocence and love, was this whole family made happy and joyful.

QUESTIONS.

Describe this scene. What did each select? The reasons given in each case? What did they then do? What effect upon their parents and the whole family?

LESSON LVII.

GOOD RESOLUTIONS.

Though I'm now in younger days,
  Nor can tell what shall befall me,
I'll prepare for every place
  Where my growing age shall call me.

Should I e'er be rich or great,
    Others shall partake my goodness;
I'll supply the poor with meat,
    Never showing scorn or rudeness.

When I see the blind or lame,
    Deaf or dumb, I'll kindly treat them;
I deserve to feel the same,
    If I mock, or hurt, or cheat them.

If I meet with railing tongues,
    Why should I return their railing?
Since I best revenge my wrongs
    By my patience never failing.

When I hear them telling lies,
    Talking foolish, cursing, swearing,
First I'll try to make them wise,
    Or I'll soon go out of hearing.

I will no one e'er offend,
    Nor be easily offended;
What's amiss I'll strive to mend,
    But endure what can't be mended.

Words of Three Syllables, Accented on the Second.

con sump tive	de fi ance	dis tur ber
con tem plate	de liv er	ex cen tric
con ten der	de lu sive	e clip tic
con tent less	de mer it	ef fec tive
con tex ture	de mol ish	e lev en
con tin gent	de mon strate	e lu sive
con tin ue	de mul cent	em bla zon
con trac ted	de mure ly	en a ble
con trib ute	de part ment	en am el
con ver gent	de part ure	en am or
con ver sant	de sert er	en clo sure
con vex ly	de spond ent	en com pass
con vey ance	des pot ic	en coun ter
con vul sive	de struc tive	en cour age
co part ner	de tach ment	en croach ment

cor rect ive	de tain der	en cum ber
cre a tive	de ter mine	en dam age
cre den da	de trun cate	en deav or
cre den tial	de vas tate	en gage ment
cyl in dric	de vel ope	en large ment
de cep tive	dis cred it	en joy ment
de ci pher	dis cum ber	en light en
de co rum	dis cov er	en li ven
de cre tal	dis cur sive	e nor mous
de duc tive	dis fig ure	en rol ment
de fect ive	dis her it	en tan gle
de fen sive	dis hon est	en vi ron

LESSON LVIII.

MAXIMS.

Good manners are not only a passport into *society*, but into the *hearts* of those with whom we associate.

Any action may produce effects over which human power has no control; nor can human sagacity foresee the end of their bearing.

If a kind word or two will render a man happy, said a French king, he must be a wretch indeed who would not gladly bestow them.

> It is a maxim in the schools
> That "Flattery" is the food of fools;"
> And whoso likes such airy meat,
> Will soon have nothing else to eat.

The youth or the man who indulges in ridiculing the little imperfections of his friends, will soon find mankind united against him.

Two of the greatest human evils are a diseased body and a discontented mind.

SPELLING BOOK.

Words of Two Syllables, Accented on the First.

ea ger	fear less	for tune	gam bler
ea gle	fear ful	free stone	gam mon
car less	fea ture	free dom	gar ment
ear ring	fee ble	fren zy	gar den
ear wig	fe male	fre quent	gar ner
earl dom	fil trate	fresh et	gar gle
ear ly	fil thy	fret ful	grand child
earth ly	fis cal	Fri day	gran ule
earth en	fla grant	friend ship	graph ic
earth born	flat ter	fris ky	grate ful
earth quake	fleet ness	froth y	grav el
earth y	flesh y	fro ward	grave ly
east er	flim sy	frus trate	gra zier
e dict	fligh ty	fud dle	grea sy
etch ing	flip pant	ful ness	great ly
e ther	flu id	ful some	great ness
eth ic	flu ent	fur bish	gre cism
eu rus	fool ish	fur nish	gree dy
e ven	foot ball	fur tive	green finch
e vil	foot path	fur ther	green gage
ex ile	force less	fur zy	greet ing
ex it	fore arm	fu ture	griev ous
eye less	fore cast	gal lant	green ness
eye brow	fore top	gain er	grind er
eye shot	fore most	gain ful	grind stone
fac tor	for ward	gain say	griz zly
faith ful	foun der	gair ish	grot to
false hood	foun dry	gal lon	grog ram
false ly	foun tain	gal lop	guile ful
fault y	four teen	gal lows	guile less

LESSON LVIX.

THE LAND ABOVE.

There is a land above,
  All beautiful and bright,
And those who love and seek the Lord
  Rise to that world of light,

There sin is known no more,
Nor tears, nor want, nor care;
There good and happy beings dwell,
And all are holy there.

THE GREEN GLASSES.

A little boy one day put on his father's green glasses. But when he had looked around him, he exclaimed: "How very strange everything looks! The sheep, and the geese, and the fences, all look green! Everything is green! What is the matter?"

His mother replied: "All the objects around you are as they were before. No change has taken place in them. The glasses thro' which you look have given them that appearance."

"And now, my son, this should teach you a good lesson. When we view things thro' the medium of envy, or hatred, or pride, or any other passion, we think they have all changed; and yet the change is in ourselves only."

"I saw a very cross, ill-natured boy, the other day, who said that everybody was cross to him, and abused him! Another boy is so proud that he thinks all other persons are mean and worthless compared with himself."

"But I know a pretty little girl who is so good-natured that nothing ever goes wrong with her. She is so cheerful and happy that everything seems to be so too. She is so joyful that all the world appears as if it were rejoicing with her."

Now, the youngest of my readers can understand this. Evil in us makes evil all around us. Good in us changes all else into goodness. Cheerfulness and kindness in us cause every thing around us to wear a cheerful and pleasant aspect.

Let me, then, exhort each of you to expel all evil feelings from your hearts, and never suffer them again to enter. They are worse than poisonous serpents. Keep the sacred fire of love toward God and man always alive in your hearts. Be kind and good to all. Look on the bright side of everything. Never murmur. Never repine. Be always thankful and cheerful.

Such a life only is worthy of rational, immortal man. It ennobles his nature, and gives him a foretaste of heaven, while yet upon the earth.

LESSON LX.

ANECDOTES.

A man by the name of Shin married a lady whose name was Foot. Their neighbors called a meeting, and rejoiced with them both that the Foot had thus *risen* in the world.

ALSO AND LIKEWISE.

A counsel once, of talents vain,
    A Quaker rudely treated,
Who in his story plain
    The word "*also*" repeated.

"Also," said Brief, with sneering wit,
    "Won't '*likewise*' do as well?"
"Nay, friend; if thou permit,
    Their difference I will tell.

Erskine's a counsel learned, we know,
    Whose talents oft surprise;
Thou art a counsel '*also*,'
    But not at all '*likewise*.'"

Words of Three Syllables, Accented on the Second.

de mon strate	a mend ment	com pul sive
a ban don	an gel ic	con cen trate
a bet tor	an nex ive	con cen tric
ab er rant	an nex ment	con cise ly
a but ment	an noy ance	con cise ness
ab hor rent	an noy er	con clu dent
ab ject ly	a noin ter	con fis cate
ab ject ness	an oth er	con clu sive
ab lep sy	ant arc tic	con cor dance
a bol ish	a part ment	con cur rence
a bor tive	a pert ly	con cur rent
a bridg ment	a pos tle	con den sate

ab rupt ly   ap par el   con dign ly
ab rupt ness   ap pa rent   con do lence
ab sor bent   co er cive   con du cive
ab ster gent   co e val   con duc tor
ab ster sive   col lu sive   con duc tress
ab strac tive   co los sus   con fes sor
ab surd ness   com mand er   con fig ure
a bun dance   com min gle   con fine ment
a but ment   com pla cent   con flex ure
a can thus   com mit tance   con form ist
ac cep ter   com mit tee   con found ed
ac cep tance   com mix ture   con ces sive
ac com plice   com po sure   con clu sive
ac com plish   com bus tive   con ver sive
ac cord ance   com plete ly   con vul sive
ac coun tant   com po nent   con vic tive
ac cou tre   com port ment   con sign ment
a bun dant   com po ser   con sis tent
ac cur sed   com po tor   con strin gent
ad emp tive   com pres sure   con struc tive

LESSON LXI.

Words Whose Meanings are the Same.

arch er   bow man   tu tor   teach er
bed lam   mad house   un guent   oint ment
alms house   poor house   ves ture   gar ment
in gress   en trance   tor por   numb ness
pot tage   por ridge   tu mor   swell ing
Sab bath   Sun day   vel lum   parch ment
que ry   ques tion   treat ment   u sage
quad rant   quar ter   ton sure   shear ing
rub bish   ru ins   fra gile   fee ble
re gent   ru ler   bale ful   wo ful
fla vor   sa vor   diz zy   gid dy
flu id   li quid   ac rid   pun gent
flex ion   ben ding   fla grant   gla ring
blos som   flow er   drea ry   dis mal

gal lows	gib bet	caus tic	burn ing
se ton	is sue	ar dent	fer vid
nap kin	tow el	fool ish	sil ly
deal er	tra der	bril liant	splen did
sci ence	knowl edge	tran script	cop y
scof fer	scorn er	spon sor	sure ty
foi ble	fail ing	sin ew	ten don
pas tor	shep herd	pli ers	pin cers

FABLE, POETRY AND SONG.

Fable and song have, in all ages, been regarded as the most pleasing and impressive modes of conveying moral truth. The author needs, therefore, make no apology for employing these methods so largely in this work, intended chiefly for the young.

THE VIPER AND THE FILE.
A FABLE.

A viper, whose caudal extremity had been crushed by a cart wheel, determined to take REVENGE *upon some other object.* Full of fury and fight, he pitched upon a large and sharp *file* which lay near him. Blow after blow he struck it with his fangs, but without making the slightest impression upon it. This but increased his rage. The file, moreover, laughed in his face, taunted him also with his crippled condition, and exclaimed:

"Oh, fie! you broken backed fool!
What rage is this that you feel?
My maker made me a tool,
To bite both iron and steel.

"When with teeth filed away,
Helpless in body you lie,
Then with what anguish you'll say,
'By my own folly I die!'"

Taunts and insults like these the viper could no longer endure. Swelling with tenfold rage, he cried:

"While teeth and strength I have,
The drama now I'll end;
With blood my body lave,
My soul to Pluto send!"

With this he struck the fatal blow, plunged his fangs deep into his sides. and, in a very short time, died, "*As the fool dieth*"—the victim of his own folly and madness.

LESSON LXII.

SONS OF PEACE.

Blest are the sons of peace,
   Whose hearts and hopes are one;
Whose kind designs to serve and please
   Thro' all their actions run.

Blest is the pious house,
   Where zeal and friendship meet;
Their songs of praise, their mingled vows,
   Make their communion sweet.

Thus on the heavenly hills,
   The saints are blest above;
Where joy, like morning dew, distills,
   And all the air is love!

THE CRABS.

Shame on you, my son, said an old crab to one of his male offspring—shame on you for moving always in that awkward sideway or backward manner. *Go straight forward!*

I shall willingly follow your advice, said his son, when I shall first see you doing the same.

MORAL.

Words are of little avail without example. First *be* and *do* what you desire to have others be and do. Then may you hope for success.

Words of Three Syllables, Accented on the First.

an ti quate	ar mor er	or re ry
an ti type	ar mo ry	har mo ny
anx ious ly	ar ro gance	bet o ny
ap a thy	ar ro gate	com pa ny
ap er ture	ar se nal	des ti ny

aph o rism	ar te ry	fel o ny
a pish ness	art ful ly	col o ny
ap o thegm	ar ti choke	beg gar y
ap an age	ar ti cle	fish er y
ap pe tence	ar ti fice	gal le ry
ap pe tite	ar ti san	gran a ry
ap ti tude	ac tu ate	witch er y
a que duct	at ti cism	bot a ny
a que ous	at ti tude	flat ter y
ar a ble	at tri bute	but ter y
ar bi ter	au di ble	pil lo ry
ar bi trate	au di ence	mem o ry
ar bo rist	au gu ry	rib ald ry
ar bo ret	au ri cle	min is try
arch er y	cen tu ry	hap pi ness
ar cu ate	cut ler y	hor ri fy
ar den cy	ef fi gy	hon es ty
ar dent ly	eb o ny	her ald ry
ar du ous	lit a ny	heb ra ist
ar go sy	lar ce ny	hom i cide
ar gu ment	tyr an ny	her e tic
a ri es	mas ter y	his to ry
arm a ment	fop pe ry	or a tor

THE ZEBRA.

How beautiful the zebra!
How pretty is his name!
But he's vicious,
And malicious,
And he cannot be made tame.

He is found in Southern Africa,
How striped is his side!
But he never
Is so clever
As to suffer you to ride.

I have heard about a Hottentot
Who caught a zebra wild;
He led him,
And he fed him,
And he loved him as a child.

He carded down his glossy hair,
But all his toil was vain;
Zebra could'nt,
Or he would'nt,
Be controlled by bit or rein.

What a shame for one so beautiful,
And outwardly so fair,
To be vicious,
And malicious,
As the pretty sometimes are!

God never smiles on beauty
When it hides a wicked heart;
Then be good here,
As you should, dear,
Lest He say at last, "Depart!"

LESSON LXIII.

THE ANT AND THE GRASSHOPPER.

A FABLE.

One day, in the winter season, a large group of ants were employed in airing and drying their supplies of corn. A grasshopper, almost dead from hunger and cold, came to them and begged that they would take pity on him, and relieve his wants by giving him a single grain of wheat or rye.

One of the ants enquired why he had not laid up food for himself during the summer as they had done.

"Alas!" said he, "I passed away my time merrily and thoughtlessly in drinking, singing and dancing, and never thought of winter."

"If that be the case," said the ant, "I can do nothing for you. *We are workers.* Idlers we never encourage. I dismiss you by reminding you of the old adage:

"They who in summer dance and sing,
In winter die of hunger's sting."

Words of Four Syllables, Accented on the Third.

ab e run cate	co ef fi cient	dis en cum ber
ad a man tine	o le an der	in ad ver tent
cat e gor ic	or tho graph ic	in ter ces sor
par a phras tic	cat e chu men	dis in her it
sci en tif ic	di e tet ic	un der ta ker
el e men tal	in ad ver tence	dis in ter ment
ep i sod ic	com pli men tal	ov er bur den
in con clu sive	hy dro stat ic	pred e ces sor
con tra dic tive	dis con cert ed	dis con tent ed
e nig mat ic	con se quen tial	un for giv ing
dem o crat ic	cir cum spec tive	mal e fac tor
an a tom ic	dis con tin ue	un for sa ken
co ex is tent	cor res pon dent	ben e fac tor
fun da men tal	in cor rect ly	as tro nom ic
cos mo log ic	dis af fect ed	par e gor ic

un im por tant	ec o nom ic	un der val ue	
in con sis tent	hy per crit ic	ev er las ting	
ab so lute ly	im ma ture ly	an ti do tal	
cal o rif ic	con ti nen tal	ret ro spec tive	
an a lep tic	man i fes to	con va les cent	

LESSON LXIV.

Spelling and Defining.

a lac ri ty	cheer ful ness	ca lum ni ate	slan der
a rid i ty	dry ness	de lib er ate	con sid er
a vid i ty	ea ger ness	en thu si ast	fa nat ic
be nef i cent	ben e fi cial	cor rob o rate	strength en
ca pit u late	sur ren der	con sol i date	so lid i fy
ce lib a cy	sin gle life	im pov er ish	pau per ize
in car cer ate	im pris on	re cip ro cate	in ter change
in ter po late	in ter line	de cap i tate	be head
pre pon der ate	over bal ance	dis en tan gle	ex tri cate
hos til i ty	en mi ty	com mem o rate	cel e brate
ca lam i ty	mis for tune	suf fi cien cy	com pe tence
va cu i ty	emp ti ness	pro gen i tor	an ces tor
re cip i ent	re ceiv er	ve rac i ty	truth ful ness
ur ban i ty	po lite ness	fe cun di ty	fruit ful ness
u til i ty	use ful ness	fe lic i ty	hap pi ness
in i qui ty	sin ful ness	dis crim i nate	dis tin guish
so lil o quy	mon o logue	sub or di nate	in fe ri or
pos ter i ty	des cend ants	a bom i nate	ab hor
fru gal i ty	par si mo ny	a nal o gy	re sem blance
lo cal i ty	res i dence	a troc i ty	bar bar i ty

THE VIOLET.

When April's warmth unlocks the clod,
Softened by gentle showers,
The violet pierces thro' the sod,
And blossoms first of flowers;
So may I give my heart to God
In childhood's early hours.

Some plants in *gardens* only found,
Are raised with pains and care;
God scatters *violets* all around,
They blossom everywhere:
Thus may my love to *all* abound,
And all my fragrance share.

Some scentless flowers stand straight and high,
With pride and hautiness;
But violets perfume land and sky,
Altho' they promise less:
Let me, with all humility,
Do more than I profess.

Sweet flower! be thou a type to me
Of blameless joy and mirth,
Of widely scattered sympathy,
Embracing all God's earth—
Of early blooming piety,
And unpretending worth.

CHAPFALLEN.

A gentleman gives it as his opinion, that the most "*down in the mouth*" of all Mr. Lincoln's Generals was Gen. Burnside, while he held his headquarters at *Falmouth*.

LESSON LXV.

A MINUTE—how soon it is flown!
And yet how important it is!
God calls every moment his own,
For all our existence is his;
And, though we may waste them in folly and play,
He notices each that we squander away.

THE ANT OR EMMET.

These emmets, how little they are in our eyes!
We tread them to dust and a troop of them dies,
Without our regard or concern;
Yet, as wise as we are, if we went to their school,
There's many a sluggard, and many a fool,
Some lessons of wisdom might learn.

They don't wear their time out in sleeping or play,
But gather up corn in a sun-shiny day,
And for winter they lay up their stores;
They manage their work in such regular forms,
One would think they foresaw all the frosts and the storms,
And so br'ot their food within doors.

But I have less sense than a poor creeping ant,
If I take not due care for the things I shall want,
Nor provide against dangers in time;
When death or old age shall stare in my face,
What a wretch shall I be at the end of my days,
If I trifle away their prime!

Now, now, while my strength and my youth are in bloom,
Let me think what shall serve me when sickness shall come,
And pray that my sins be forgiven;
Let me read in good books, and believe and obey,
That when death turns me out of this cottage of clay,
I may dwell in a palace in heaven!

Words of Three Syllables, Accented on the First.

can o py	dep u ty	bit ter ness
pan o ply	del i cate	ben e fice
tap es try	dis si pate	big a mist
ten e ment	dom i nant	big ot ed
van i ty	det ri ment	bla zon ry
vis i ble	del e gate	ed i fy
vic to ry	dul ci fy	ed it or
vig or ous	dec i mate	ed u cate
vis it or	cal cu late	ef fa ble
par i ty	cal i co	em u late
per ju ry	cap i tal	el e gy
per se cute	cap ti vate	el e ment
plen ti ful	cer ti fy	el e phant
per quis ite	con fi dent	em a nate
pol y glot	cop per y	em e ry
prop er ty	cop u late	em i grant
pov er ty	cop y ist	em bro cate
pen u ry	cor o nal	em e rald
pur ga tive	cor o ner	em i grate
pun ish ment	com e dy	em i nent
quack e ry	cor mo rant	ep i cure
quer u lous	cor ne ous	en er gy
quid di ty	cor di al	en er gize
quick sil ver	cor net cy	en fi lade
rad i cal	cor po rate	en ter prise

rad i cate	cor pu lent	er e mite
ram i fy	ban ish ment	er ror ist
rap tu rous	bap tis try	er u dite
ran cor ous	bar ba rism	es ti mate
rar i fy	bar ba rize	es ti val
rav en ous	bar be cue	fam i ly
def er ence	bar ber ry	fab u lous
dil i gent	bar ley corn	fab ri cate
dig ni ty	ben e fit	fab u list
dim i ty	big a my	fac to ry

LESSON LXVI.

THE THIEF.

Why should I deprive my neighbor
  Of his goods against his will?
Hands were made for honest labor,
  Not to plunder or to steal.

'Tis a foolish self-deceiving
  By such tricks to hope for gain;
All that's ever got by thieving
  Turns to sorrow, shame and pain.

Have not Eve and Adam taught us
  Their sad profit to compute?
To what dismal state they brought us,
  When they stole forbidden fruit!

Oft we see a young beginner
  Practice little pilfering ways;
Till grown up a hardened sinner,
  The gallows ends his days.

Theft will not be always hidden,
  Though we fancy none can spy;
When we take a thing forbidden,
  God beholds it with His eye.

Guard my heart, O God of heaven!
  Lest I covet what's not mine;
Lest I steal what is not given,
  Guard my heart and hand from sin.

THE POLITICIANS.

Two political parties were passing each other, going to their respective places of meeting. Much caustic wit and dry humor passed between them. Said one of them to his friend: "George, what do you think? My horse, back yonder, was such a fool that he wanted to turn and go with your party, but I would not allow it." "Why," said George, "I think he clearly showed that, like Baalam's ass, he had more sense than his rider."

Words of Two Syllables, Accented on the Second.

gen teel	re pine	en dear	un sown
glo bose	de sist	en twine	un worn
gran tee	de fray	de fine	un wept
gran tor	un say	dif fuse	un told
grim ace	at tain	sur mount	en close
har poon	en twine	re lume	con sole
mon soon	con sign	do main	six teen
re vise	con clude	ex plain	sus tain
ca rouse	la ment	pre pare	un teach
tri une	le gume	dis train	re hearse
re bate	se cure	suc ceed	re search
in flate	se crete	sur round	ro bust
sa lute	col lude	at tain	re mark
pre pare	ex plain	at tempt	un mask
en snare	ex pose	be hest	un seen
de sire	e lope	be hoove	bas soon
dis may	es cape	de ceit	im pugn
bal loon	en close	a light	de note

LESSON LXVII.

REVERENTIAL PRAISE.

Before Jehovah's awful throne,
  Ye nations bow with sacred joy;
Know that the Lord is God alone,
  He can create and He destroy.

D*

His sovereign power, without our aid,
  Made us of clay and formed us men;
And when, like wandering sheep, we strayed,
  He brought us to His fold again.

We are His people, we His care,
  Our souls and all our mortal frame;
What lasting honors shall we rear,
  Almighty Maker, to Thy name!

We'll crowd Thy gates with thankful songs,
  High as the heavens our voices raise;
And earth, with her ten thousand tongues,
  Shall fill Thy courts with sounding praise.

Wide as the world is Thy command,
  Vast as eternity Thy love;
Firm as a rock Thy truth shall stand,
  When rolling years shall cease to move!

Words of Three Syllables, Accented on the First.

cit a del	cow ard ly	gar ni ture
clem en cy	cras si tude	gar ri son
cler i cal	cred i ble	gel a tine
cod i cil	cred it or	gel id ness
con so nant	cred u lous	gem in ous
con sta ble	crim i nal	gen er al
con stan cy	crit ic al	gen er ate
con sti pate	crock er y	gen er ous
con sti tute	croc o dile	gen e sis
con ti nent	cru ci al	ge ni al
con tra band	crus ti ly	gen i tive
con tra ry	cu bit al	ge ni us
con vo cate	cul min ate	gen u ine
cop i er	cul ti vate	glo ri fy
co pi ous	cul pa ble	gloss a ry
cor o nal	feb ri fuge	gov ern or
cor po rate	fec u lent	gov ern ess
cor pu lence	fed er al	grad u ate
cos mic al	fed er ate	gran u late

cost li ness	fel o ny	graph ic al
cot ta ger	flat ter y	grass i ness
coun sel lor	flat u ous	grat i fy
coun te nance	for ti fy	gra ting ly
coun ter part	for tu nate	grat u late
coun ter sign	ful mi nate	grav i ty
cour te ous	fu mi gate	grav i tate
cour te sy	fur be low	greed i ness
cov e nant	fur tive ly	grid i ron
cov er ing	gal le ry	grit ti ness
cov er let	gal ax y	hab it ant
cov et ous	gal li cism	hab i tude

LESSON LXVIII.

THE SOUL.

The soul, of origin divine,
God's glorious image, freed from clay,
In heaven's eternal sphere shall shine
    A star of day!

The sun is but a spark of fire,
A transient meteor in the sky;
The soul, immortal as its sire,
    Shall never die.

THE SLUGGARD.

The voice of the sluggard, I hear him complain,
"You have waked me too soon, I must slumber again;"
As the door on his hinges, so he on his bed,
Turns his sides, and his shoulders, and his heavy head.

"A little more sleep, a little more slumber,"
Thus he wastes half his days, and his hours without number;
And when he gets up he sits folding his hands,
Or walks about sauntering, or trifling he stands.

I passed by his garden, and saw the wild brier,
The thorn and the thistle, grow broader and higher;
The clothes that hung on him are turning to rags,
And his money still wastes till he starves or he begs.

I made him a visit, still hoping to find
He had taken more care for improving his mind;
He told me his dreams, talked of eating and drinking,
But he scarce reads his bible and never loves thinking.

Said I then to my heart, "Here's a lesson for me!
That man's but a picture of what I might be;
But thanks to my friends for their care in my breeding,
Who taught me betimes to love working and reading."

Words of Four Syllables, Accented on the Third.

math e mat ics	in de ci sion	re in force ment
con va les cent	in se cure ly	met a phys ics
re im burse ment	in co he rent	dis con tent ment
re com mence ment	ir re spec tive	met a mor phose
in de pend ent	su per struc ture	mis in ter pret
om ni pres ent	mis de mean or	cir cum ja cent
pre ex is tent	mis be hav ior	dis a gree ment
in at ten tive	ap pa ra tus	dis en tan gle
sup ple men tal	per ad ven ture	in ef fec tive
in ter mit tent	ef flo res cent	pes ti len tial
or na men tal	in con clu sive	prov i den tial
sac ra men tal	in con sis tent	su per struc ture
in ter mar ry	bas ti na do	ar o mat ic
ac ci den tal	ac ci den tal	e nig mat ic
o ver la den	an i mad vert	e go tis tic
o ri en tal	in ci den tal	re con sid er
reg i men tal	in con des cence	over bur den
hor i zon tal	man u fac ture	hyp o crit ic
an a lyt ic	af fi da vit	his tri on ic
on te mun dane	dis a vow al	com pli men tal
des pe ra do	in stru men tal	el e men tal
en ter tain ment	mon u men tal	

LESSON LXIX.

JEWELS.

Some ladies are fond of showing jewels made of diamonds and gold. A Roman lady once had two sons whom she had reared with great care. She valued them above all price. While ladies of fashion were dis-play-ing their fine clothes and costly jewels abroad, she was at home training up her sons in the way they should go.

When asked where and what her jewels were, she presented her noble sons and said : " These are my jewels." Children, you little know the value of such mothers. You should honor them highly, and strive to become jewels such as Rome never produced—at once the joy of your parents and the honor and glory of your country.

THE LORD'S PRAYER.

Our Father who art in heaven. Hallowed be Thy name Thy kingdom come. Thy will be done in earth as it is in heaven. Give us this day our daily bread. And forgive us our debts as we forgive our debtors. And lead us not into temptation, but deliver us from evil; for thine is the kingdom, the power, and the glory forever. Amen !

Words of Three Syllables Accented on the First.

cu mu late	det ri ment	eq ua ble
cu ra tive	dif fer ent	e qual ize
cu ri ous	dif fi cult	e qui nox
cur ri cle	dif flu ent	cre mite
cur so ry	dis cre pant	es cu lent
cur va ted	ear nest ly	es tim ate
cur va ture	earth i ness	es ti val
cur vi ty	ea si ly	eth ic al
cus tom er	ea si ness	eu lo gy
cus to dy	eas ter ly	eu pho ny
cu ti cle	eat a ble	e ven ing
cyn ic al	eb o ny	ev er green
dan ger ous	ec sta cy	ev i dent
de cen cy	ed u cate	e vil ness
dec o rate	ef fi gy	ev i tate
del i cate	e go tism	ex ca vate
def in ite	eg lan tine	ex e crate
del e gate	e go tise	ex e cute
del i cate	ef flu ent	ex i gence
dem a gogue	el e vate	ex or cise
dem i god	el o quence	ex pe dite
dem o crat	em a nate	ex ple tive

dep u rate	ed i fy	ex quis ite
dep u ty	ed i ble	ex u date
der o gate	en ter prise	eye wit ness
des o late	ep i cure	fab u lest
des pe rate	ep i logue	fab u lous
des ti ny	ep i thet	fac ul ty
des ti tute	ep i taph	fal la cy

LESSON LXX.

PROVERBS.

The comforter's head never aches.
The covetous man is his own tormentor.
The crow thinks her young ones the fairest.
The eye of the master does more than his hands.
The faulty stands on his guard.
The foremost dog catches the hare.
The man of threatened life lives long.
The gray mare is the better horse.

THE WISE CHOICE.

King Sol-o-mon of old
    A hap-py choice had made;
'Twas not for life, 'twas not for gold,
    Nor hon-or that he pray-ed.

He chose that bet-ter part,
    That leads to heav-en-ly joys—
A wise and un-der-stand-ing heart,
    And God ap-prov-ed the choice.

If this is what we seek,
    We can-not ask a-miss;
The young-est, poor-est child may speak,
    And ask the Lord for this.

Words of Two Syllables, Accented on the First, in which ow have the long sound of o, as in note.

bar row	hal low	bur row	swal low
fil low	fel low	har row	fur row
cal low	yar row	win dow	ar row
tal low	fol low	nar row	wil low
el bow	far row	mor row	yel low
hol low	mead ow	spar row	mel low
bel low	mal low	win ow	ful low
min now	shad ow	wid ow	sor row

Words of Two Syllables, Accented on the First, in which A sounds as in fall.

plau dit	pal try	daugh ter	wal nut
wa ter	saw yer	saw pit	quar ter
law yer	want ing	flaw y	haw thorn
braw ny	draw ing	slaugh ter	al most
au thor	sau cer	au ger	cau sey
au tumn	faul ty	mau ger	pau per
maud lin	gau dy	al ter	sau cy
pal sy	draw ers	fal ter	taw ny
draw ers	mawk ish	pal ter	drawl ing

LESSON LXXI.

LIVE FOR SOMETHING.

Live for something, be not idle,
    Look about thee for employ;
Sit not down to useless dreaming,
    Labor is the sweetest joy.
Folded hands are ever weary,
    Selfish hearts are never gay;
Life for thee hath many duties,
    Active be, then, while you may.

Scatter blessings in thy pathway,
    Gentle words and cheering smiles
Better are than gold and silver,
    With their grief-dispelling wiles.

As the pleasant sunshine falleth,
　Ever on the grateful earth,
So let sympathy and kindness
　Gladden well the darkened hearth.

Hearts there are oppressed and weary;
　Drop the tear of sympathy,
Whisper words of hope and comfort,
　Give, and thy reward shall be
Joy to thy soul, returning
　From this perfect fountain head;
Freely as thou givest
　Shall the grateful light be shed.

Words of Four Syllables, Accented on the First.

ac cu ra cy	car i ca ture	bal ne a ry
am i ca ble	col or a ble	ac tu a ry
am or ous ly	nec es sa ry	lu min a ry
ac cu rate ness	ex cel len cy	mo men ta ry
ad di to ry	com pe ten cy	mod er ate ly
am pli fi er	con ti nen cy	ap pe ten cy
cu li na ry	cor ol la ry	sed en ta ry
mo ment a ry	cor ri gi ble	mil i ta ry
nu ga to ry	cov et ous ness	ar bi tra ry
nu mer a ry	dec re to ry	form u la ry
a mi a ble	dic tion a ry	for tu nate ly
es ti ma ble	drom e da ry	lit er a ry
an cil la ry	im po ten cy	pul mo na ry
an i ma tive	med ul la ry	em is sa ry
bre vi a ry	par ce na ry	mis cel la ny
del i ca cy	im i ta ble	dif fi dent ly
con tu ma cy	cer e mo ny	dif fi cul ty
an nu la ry	cu mu la tive	dil i gent ly
an te cham ber	ali mo ny	ad e quate ly
ob sti na cy	an ti mo ny	an swer a ble
ex i gen cy	mat ri mo ny	sal u ta ry
a pi a ry	hon or a ry	dil a to ry
ap o plex y	sec on da ry	cap il la ry
feu da to ry	preb en da ry	man da to ry

LESSON LXXII.

WEALTH AND POVERTY.

Can he who with the tide of fortune sails,
  More pleasures from the sweets of nature share;
Do zephyrs waft him more ambrosial gales,
  Or do his groves a gayer livery wear?

To me the heavens unveil as pure a sky,
  To me the flowers as rich a bloom disclose,
The morning beams as radiant to mine eye,
  And darkness guides me to as sweet repose.

If luxury their lavish dainties piles,
  And still attends upon their stated hours.
Doth health reward them with her open smiles,
  Or exercise enlarge their feeble powers?

'Tis not in richest mines of Indian gold
  That man this jewel, happiness, can find;
If his unfeeling breast, to virtue cold,
  Denies her entrance to his ruthless mind.

Wealth, pomp and honor are but gaudy toys,
  Alas! how poor the pleasures they impart;
Virtue's the sacred source of all the joys
  That claim a lasting mansion in the heart.

TREASURES.

Lay not up treasures for yourselves upon earth, where moth and rust do corrupt, and where thieves break through and steal. But lay up for yourselves treasures in heaven, where neither moth nor rust doth corrupt, and where thieves do not break through nor steal; for where your treasure is there will your heart be also.—*Bible.*

Words of Six Syllables, Accented on the Fourth.

ac cep ti bil i ty	com pat i bil i ty	in vol u bil i ty
ac count a bil i ty	en cy clo pe di a	e jac u la to ry
a mi a bil i ty	in com pre hen si ble	in sen si bil i ty
ex tem po ra ne ous	re sis ti bil i ty	im prob a bil i ty
a pol o get ic al	un pop u lar i ty	an te me rid i an

ap pli ca bil i ty	in flam ma bil i ty	im mu ta bil i ty
a poc a lyp ti cal	in com pre hen si ble	in cred i bil i ty
ma te ri al i ty	ir reg u lar i ty	an ti scor bu ti cal
dis ad van ta geous	de fen si bil i ty	im pos si bil i ty
in fal li bil i ty	mal le a bil i ty	in tan gi bil i ty
in fu si bil i ty	in fe ri or i ty	a math e mat i cal
ec cle si as ti cal	per cep ti bil i ty	ac cus tom a ri ly
an te ri or i ty	il le gi bil i ty	in ca pa bil i ty
am bi dex ter i ty	di vis i bil i ty	in flex i bil i ty
do struc ti bil i ty	un phil o soph ic al	il lib er al i ty
im per son al i ty	con ge ni al i ty	in fran gi bil i ty
gu ber na to ri al	u ni ver sal i ty	in hos pi tal i ty
com pres si bil i ty	ir rec on ci la ble	im pres si bil i ty

LESSON LXXIII.

PROVERBS.

The dime is ill saved that shames its master.
The hasty hand catches frogs for fish.
The highest branch is not the safest roost.
Fly pleasure and it will follow you.
Forgive any one sooner than yourself.
Faint heart never won fair lady.
Fools tie knots and wise men loose them.
Plenty of thistles, plenty of prickles.
Give a dog an ill name and hang him.
Give a fool rope and he hangs himself.

THE ROSE.

How fair is the rose! what a beautiful flower!
   The glory of April and May!
But the leaves—how soon do they fade in the bower!
   See! they wither and die in a day.

But the rose has one powerful virtue to boast,
   Above other flowers of the field;
When the leaves are all dead, and the colors are lost,
   Still how sweet a perfume it will yield!

So frail is the youth and the beauty of men,
   Though they bloom and look gay like the rose;
But all our fond care to preserve them is vain,
   Time kills them as fast as he goes.

Then I'll not be proud of my youth or my beauty,
Since both of them wither and fade;
But gain a *good name* by well doing my duty,
This will scent like a rose when I'm dead.

Words of Three Syllables, Accented on the Second.

a muse ment	at tor ney	ex ot ic
a mu sive	en ven om	ex pec tance
a mass ment	en vi ron	ex plo sive
a na nas	en cum ber	ex po sure
ap pren tice	pre sump tive	ex pound er
ap prov al	re dun dant	ex pres sive
ap prove ment	pro cure ment	ex pro brate
a quat ic	com mit ment	ex pul sive
arch bish op	com min gle	ex sic cate
a ro ma da	cre a tive	ex tal ic
ar men tal	pe ru sal	ex ter nal
ar raign ment	in vec tive	ex tin guish
ar range ment	im pul sive	ex tir pate
ar rear age	de liv er	ex treme ly
ar ri val	de duce ment	ex ult ant
au ro ra	hor rif ic	for get ful
au then tic	ho mer ic	for giv ing
a ven ger	en ti tle	ge ner ic
back sli der	e rup tive	ge ne va
be diz zen	er rat ic	ig no ble
be drag gle	es tab lish	ex ple tive
be gin ner	e ter nal	es cape ment
be hold er	e van id	re fu sal
be la bor	e va sive	in tend ant
be la ted	e vent ful	neg lect ful
be lea guer	ex act ive	pro duc tive
be liev er	ex am ine	pre ten der
oi den tal	ex am ple	im pres sive
do tan ic	ex clu sive	per sua sive
bra va do	ex car nate	sub mis sive
e ru men	ex cep tive	mo men tous
re cov er	ex cheq uer	pro gres sive
for get ful	ex cite ment	re ten tive

fi nan cial	ex clu´ sive	se lec ted
sa tan ic	ex cre tive	of fen sive
for got ten	ex cur sive	re ver sive
be sot ted	ex em plar	per spec tive
a ver ment	ex hib it	pro tru sive

LESSON LXXIV.

THE OWL AND THE MOUSE.

A FABLE.

An owl was caught in a snare. In this sad condition he entreated a mouse to gnaw off the cords and liberate him. The mouse refused to do so, unless the owl would first solemnly promise never again to kill mice.

The owl was liberated on that condition. Not long afterwards he caught a *bat* in an old barn, and was about to devour it. But being struck with its resemblance to the mouse, he hesitated about killing it. At length he concluded to devour it as a *bird*, and not as a mouse.

MORAL.

The principle with many persons is, "Change the name and you may do what you like." Thus murder is defended as *duelling*. Theft and robbery are lauded under the name of "*sharp trading!*" Do wicked men hate religion and desire to make it odious? They give it the name hypocrisy or priestcraft, and then they spit at it all their venom, and pile upon it all their abuse!

Words of Two Syllables, Accented on the First, in each of which TH *have their asperate sound.*

an ther	au thor	thirs ty	diph thong
e ther	meth od	thim ble	triph thong
eth ics	pan ther	thick et	thin ly
ze nith	length y	thrif ty	thor ough
the sis	Thurs day	throt tle	thros tle
thun der	think er	sab bath	ja cinth
an them	death less	thou sand	filth y

Words of Three Syllables, and Words of Four Syllables, Accented on the First and Second, in which TH *have the asperate sound.*

a can thus	am a ranth	ther mom e ter
ca thar tic	am e thyst	can thar i des
me theg lin	math e sis	phi lan thro py
me thod ic	syn the sis	the ol o gy
pan the on	ap a thy	an tith e sis
au then tic	leth ar gy	an tip a thy
syn thet ic	lab y rinth	a nath e ma
ca the dral	hy a cinth	mis an thro py
par thet ic	ep i thet	the oc ra cy
u re thra	ap o thegm	the od o lite
ath let ic	en thusiasm	me thod i cal
un think ing	me thod i cal	e the re al
en throne ment	a rith me tic	the ri a cal
de throne ment	co rin thi an	au then ti cate
tho rac ic	li thot o my	au thor i ty
un thrif ty	ca thol i con	le vi a than
un thwart ed	hy poth e sis	hy poth e cate
un thank ful	my thol o gy	un truth ful ness
cath o lic	or thog ra phy	un think ing ly
pleth o ric	li thog ra phy	ath let i cal

LESSON LXXV.

FLOWERS.

Yes; flowers have tones—God gave to each
A language of its own,
And bade the simple blossom teach,
Where'er its seeds are sown;
His voice is on the mountain height,
And by the river's side,
Where flowers blush in glowing light,
In loneliness or pride;
We feel all o'er the blooming sod,
It is the language of our God.

PROVERBS.

Silence seldom does any harm.
Sit in your place and none will make you rise.
Speak the truth and shame the devil.
Short reckonings make long friends.
Sloth is the mother of poverty.
Speech is the gift of all—thought of few.
Such is the tree, such the fruit.
Soon ripe, soon rotten. Soon well, soon ill.
Take care of the dimes—dollars then are safe.
Take heed and surely speed.
Tell me your companions—that is enough
Temperance is the best physic.
That is well spoken that is well taken.
That's placing the cart before the horse.
The blind man's wife needs no painting.
The cobbler's wife is the worst shod.

Words of Different Accent.

Many words, alike in spelling, are distinguished only by the accent. In the following lesson, the nouns and adjectives of the first and third columns have the accent on the first syllable. The verbs, in the second and fourth columns, have it on the second:

affix	affix	absent	absent
accent	accent	augment	augment
abstract	abstract	cement	cement
compound	compound	colleague	colleague
collect	collect	convert	convert
conduct	conduct	conduct	conduct
confine	confine	consort	consort
conserve	conserve	contract	contract
conflict	conflict	contest	contest
concert	concert	converse	converse
convict	convict	convoy	convoy
digest	digest	ferment	ferment
extract	extract	import	import
export	export	frequent	frequent

impress	impress	gallant	gallant
incense	incense	insult	insult
concrete	concrete	attribute	attribute
record	record	rebel	rebel
refuse	refuse	subject	subject
survey	survey	surname	surname
transfer	transfer	torment	torment
transport	transport	upcast	upcast

LESSON LXXVI.

THE CONFLICT ENDED.

Servant of God, well done!
  Rest from thy loved employ;
The battle fought, the victory won,
  Enter thy Master's joy.

His sword was in his hand,
  Still warm with recent fight,
Ready, that moment, at command,
  Thro' rock and steel to smite.

Oft with its fiery edge
  His arm had quelled the foe,
And laid, resistless in its course,
  The demon armies low.

At midnight came the cry,
  "Come, take a higher sphere;"
He woke and saw his Captain nigh,
  Then strong in faith and prayer.

His spirit with a bound,
  Left its encumbering clay;
His tent, at sunrise, on the ground,
  An empty ruin lay!

Servant of God, well done!
  Praise be thy new employ;
And while eternal ages run,
  Rest in thy SAVIOR'S joy!

Words of Three Syllables, Accented on the Second.

a bate ment	con clu sive	en slave ment
en rol ment	de fi ant	re ten tive
en large ment	em bar go	ro man tic
en tan gle	em bar rass	tor men tor
in her it	em bit ter	en coun ter
de file ment	ac knowl edge	sur ren der
in duce ment	op po nent	fo ren sic
en camp ment	op po ser	for bid ding
de cep tive	ab sor bent	sple net ic
co part ner	of fen sive	spe cif ic
pre fer ment	ab jure ment	pe dan tic
con fine ment	as sua sive	se ques ter
ac quit tal	ac cus tom	sub scri ber
e quip ment	ac cou tre	de liv er
af firm ance	co e qual	en rap ture
de ter gent	co e val	en force ment
di min ish	con tent ment	in for mal
de ben ture	sub mis sive	pre fer ment
dis cred it	sub ver sive	pro lif ic
do mes tic	re fine ment	pros pec tive
do min ion	re li ance	tri um phant
de mer it	re cum bent	re bel lious
cos met ic	se cern ment	re plev in
en deav or	se duc tive	oc cur rence
in form ant	de liv er	ac cred it
a bu sive	de struc tive	a mal gam
as sign ment	de throne ment	ad mon ish

LESSON LXXVII.

GOD'S PRESENCE AND GLORY.

God came from Teman, and the Holy One from Mount Paran. Selah. His glory covered the heavens, and the earth was full of His praise. His brightness was as the light. He had horns coming out of his hand, and there was the hiding out of His power. Before Him went the pestilence, and burning coals went forth at his feet. He stood and measured the earth; He beheld and drove asunder the nations, and the everlasting mountains were scattered, the perpetual hills did bow; His ways are everlasting.

I saw the tents of Cushan in affliction; and the curtains of the land of Midian did tremble.

Was the Lord displeased against the rivers? Was thine anger against the rivers? Was Thy wrath against the sea, that Thou didst ride upon Thy horses and Thy chariots of salvation?

Thy bow was made quite naked, according to the oaths of the tribes, even Thy word. Selah.

The mountains saw Thee, and they trembled; the deep uttered his voice, and lifted up his hands on high. The sun and the moon stood still in their habitations; at the light of Thine arrows they went, and at the shining of Thy glittering spear.

Thou didst march through the land in indignation; Thou didst thresh the heathen in anger; Thou wentest forth for the salvation of Thy people, even for the salvation of Thine anointed.—*Bible.*

Words terminating in IZE, *Accented on the First Syllable.*

bot a nize	bar bar ize	gal van ize
civ il ize	ro man ize	bru tal ize
bas tard ize	dog ma tize	col o nize
sub si dize	fer til ize	i dol ize
det o nize	tyr an nize	re al ize
gor mand ize	mor al ize	gal van ize
her bo rize	em pha size	le gal ize
mag net ize	mod ern ize	pul ver ize
stig ma tize	mem or ize	mel o dize
the o rize	lo cal ize	po lar ize
jour nal ize	ster il ize	fo cal ize
cau ter ize	gar ga rize	vo cal ize
pat ron ize	tan tal ize	sat ir ize
ox yd ize	or gan ize	os tra cize
ju da ize	chris tian ize	tem por ize
can on ize	au thor ize	gen til ize
ag o nize	dram a tize	scru ti nize

Note.—The terminations *ing, ed* and *ation* should be added to each of these words as they are spelled.

E

TROUT AND YOUTH.

It is said that trout are often caught with hooks in their mouths, which they had carried off only a short time before!

This is not strange to those who reflect that juveniles of the human family will swallow the same *hook* a thousand times! They do this also with the known fact before them, that "*Caught at last*" is always the death-knell report!

LESSON LXXVIII.

EARLY DEVOTION.

Early, my God, without delay,
  I haste to seek Thy face;
My thirsty spirit faints away,
  Without Thy cheering grace.

So pilgrims on the scorching sand,
  Beneath a burning sky,
Long for a cooling stream at hand,
  And they must drink or die.

I've seen Thy glory and Thy power,
  Thro' all Thy temple shine!
My God, repeat that heavenly hour,
  That vision so divine.

Not all the blessings of a feast
  Can please my soul so well,
As when Thy richer grace I taste,
  And in Thy presence dwell.

Not life itself, with all its joys,
  Can my best passions move,
Or raise so high my cheerful voice,
  As Thy forgiving love.

Thus, till my last expiring day,
  I'll bless my God and King;
Thus will I lift my hands to pray,
  And tune my lips to sing.

Words of Five Syllables, Accented on the Third.

ac a dem ic al	hy dro ceph a lus	in ca pac i tate
en er get ic al	im me chan i cal	in can des cen cy
e nig mat ic al	im me mo ri al	in ef fi cient ly
met a phor ic al	il le git i mate	fu si bil i ty
ac a do mi an	im me thod ic al	fri a bil i ty
am phi the a tre	ap o the o sis	di a met ri cal
il le gal i ty	el e men ta ry	in ter me di ate
an e mom e ter	ep i log ic al	in cor rupt i ble
am o ni a cal	ex com mu ni cate	in dis crim i nate
an e mog ra phy	fu si bil i ty	im pro pri e ty
in cre du li ty	aph o ris ti cal	in ex pe di ent
par si mo ni ous	en er get i cal	in com pat i ble
gram i niv or ous	hy per crit i cal	in de ci sive ly
cu ri os i ty	im mo bil i ty	ho mo ge ne ous
in ac ces si ble	im ma te ri al	ac ri mo ni ous
in sig nif i cant	im mor tal i ty	e qui pon der ate
dis pro por tion ate	im per cep ti ble	un ac cep ti ble
am bi gu i ty	im mar ces si ble	in ad mis si ble
con tra ri e ty	im per sua si ble	in ter nun ti o
an ti typ i cal	im por tu ni ty	par ti cip i al
ar o mat i cal	im pro lif i cate	in ef fec tu al
ep i gram ma tist	al i men ta ry	ef flo res cen cy
ep i sod ic al	in ar tic u late	in dis pen sa ble
aph i lan tho py	na tion al i ty	in ter cal a ry

LESSON LXXIX.

GRATITUDE.

What shall I render to my God
  For all his kindness shown?
My feet shall visit Thine abode,
  My songs address Thy throne!

Among the saints that fill Thy house,
  My offerings shall be paid;
There shall my zeal perform the vows
  My soul in anguish made.

Now I am Thine, forever Thine,
  Nor shall my purpose move;
Thy hands have loosed my bonds of pain,
  And bound me with Thy love.

Various Monosyllables.

stride	sprite	stoop	rough
guide	smite	troop	tough
sword	barge	crump	dodge
gourd	charge	trump	podge
lewd	sheen	twist	trash
shrewd	screen	wrist	splash
crouch	quaff	dose	meek
slouch	laugh	gross	sleek
grove	burst	loose	small
strove	worst	goose	scrawl
pouch	launch	snare	clothe
vouch	craunch	square	loathe

NATURAL HISTORY is at once very pleasing and instructive to children and youth. It treats of the entire animal kingdom, which you may know includes all the beasts, birds, fishes, reptiles, insects and the animalculæ, too small to be seen without the aid of the microscope.

It is very delightful to see or to read about all the different animals, to learn their classifications, and become acquainted with their size, their appearance, their structure, their disposition, their manner of life, and the uses which they may subserve in the world.

In this little work I can give you only a few specimens; but I hope you will take an interest in all of God's wonderful works, and get acquainted with as many of them as you can.

Here is a very curious little creature, called the "Red Owl." His eyes and his ears are very wonderful. And then the manner in which he doles out his notes is very queer. You need never be afraid of owls. They do not hurt people, nor do they forbode any evil to us when they come about our houses.

THE RED OWL.

Owls are birds of prey, and the only birds of that sort that are nocturnal in their habits—that is, which sleep through the day, and move about and seek their prey at night. To enable them to find their way in the dark, and see their prey—even down to small mice—their eyes are very large, and the pupil is extraordinarily large, so as to let in a great amount of what little light there may be shining in the night. At the same time, there is a circle, almost funnel-shaped, of light feathers, surrounding the eye, and so disposed as to throw light upon the eye. Then its ears are very large, (it is the *only* bird that has an external ear) and very sensitive. In some sorts of owls the ear has a lid, which opens at the will of the bird; and so its sense of hearing is perhaps as important a help to it as its sight is in catching its prey in the dark. Besides these qualifications for the peculiar life they lead, their plumage is so downy that when they fly they make no noise, which enables them to pounce upon the little mouse or rabbit before the victim is aware of his danger.

The red owl is known in this country as the little screech-owl. Did you never hear their querulous, melancholy voice in the evening? On moonlight nights they seem to take delight in making the country road lonesome by answering each other across the fields.

They sleep in the day time in cedar, pine and other thick trees, and generally build in the hollows of trees, but sometimes in orchards.

LESSON LXXX.

HEALTH AND BEAUTY.

A maiden once, well known to fame,
    With rosy cheek and beaming eye,
When questioned whence her beauty came,
    Thus promptly made in rhyme reply:

"O'er beauteous grounds I've daily walked,
    Where buds and flowers their glories spread;
With them, as friend to friend, I've talked,
    And on their richest fragrance fed.

"Where Nature grouped her magic bowers,
    And breathed Elysian sweets around,
There have I spent my leisure hours,
    And there my chief delight have found.

> "My mind is ever active, bright,
>   True wisdom's teachings make me wise;
> Each winged hour brings fresh delight,
>   And thence both 'Health' and 'Beauty' rise."
>
> "Enough, enough," her friend replied,
>   "The ample causes now I view;
> My in-door life I'll lay aside,
>   And your example I'll pursue."
>
> And now, ye Southern ladies fair,
>   Would you to those attainments rise?
> *Live much in fresh and open air,*
>   *Eve's ancient duties ne'er despise.*—B.

In the following lists of Words, Monosyllables and Dissyllables, the sound of H *precedes that of the* W, *hwen hwat.*

whale	which	whee dle	whi tish
what	whisk	white wash	whi ting
wharf	whiff	whip stock	whis per
wheat	whim	whis key	whis ker
wheel	whip	wher ry	whith er
wheeze	whin	whet stone	whis tle
while	why	whith er	whif fle
whine	whiz	whit low	whit tle
white	whelm	whig gish	whig gism
whit	when	whim per	whin ny
whelp	whist	whirl pool	whirl wind
whence	whey	whin yard	whil bat
where	whig	whip graft	wharf age

EXAMPLES FOR CONFEDERATE LADIES.

An English traveler, who has had opportunities of observation in the first circles in the various American States, North and South, expresses his astonishment at the indolence of American fine ladies.

He says no English woman of rank, from the queen downward, would remain unemployed for half an hour, or sit in a rocking-chair, unless seriously ill. With hardly an exception, he says, they copy the business letters of their husbands, fathers or brothers, attend minutely to the wants of the poor, taking part in their amusements and sympathizing with their sorrows, visit and superintend the schools, work in their gardens, see to their household concerns, look over the weekly accounts, and with all their occupations, by early hours keep up their acquaintance with the literature and politics of the day, and cultivate the accomplishments of music and drawing, living lives of energy and usefulness, without ostentation or an idea that they are doing more than their simple duty.

LESSON LXXXI.

WHO SHALL INHABIT?

Who shall inhabit in Thy hill,
  O God of holiness?
Whom will the Lord admit to dwell
  So near His throne of grace?

The man who walks in pious ways,
  And works with righteous hands;
Who trusts his Maker's promised grace,
  And follows his commands.

LOOK UPWARD.

A man, whose memory was so short that he could not remember the eighth commandment, went one night to his neighbor's field to steal corn.

He took his little son with him to hold the sacks, and assist in the intended robbery.

Before entering the field he stood upon the fence, and looked in every direction round him to see if any person was watching them. Supposing that no one observed them, he got down and started toward the corn-heap. His son, who had been well taught in the Sabbath school, said to him: "Father, there is one way you did not look." "What way?" said he. "Why you forgot to look *upward.*"

Conscience smitten, and in terror at the thought of that all-penetrating eye that was upon him, he instantly withdrew from the field; and, it is said, never afterwards was guilty of a like offense.

"*Look upward*" is a good motto. All persons should remember it.

Words of Four Syllables, Accented on the Second.

ad ven tu rous	ir res o lute	ma lev o lent
ad ver si ty	pre em i nent	i tin er ant
un gen er ous	e mol u ment	hy drog ra phy
mag nan i mous	dis par age ment	ich nog ra phy
im pos tu mate	en cour age ment	im mac u late
im pose a ble	es tab lish ment	im man a cle
im pres si ble	em bel lish ment	im man i ty
om nip o tent	em bod i ment	im me di ate
mi nor i ty	en fran chise ment	il lau da ble
mel lif lu ent	im pros per ous	il lit er ate
in car cer ate	im mor tal ize	im pol i tic
in an i mate	im mod er ate	sym met ri cal
im prov i dence	ve rac i ty	som nif er ous
im por tu nate	ve nal i ty	vo lu min ous
in teg u ment	fe cun di ty	mor tif er ous
as ton ish ment	fu ne re al	ar mig er ous
re lin quish ment	im prob a ble	ar mip o tent
im pris on ment	in noc u ous	al tim e try
ir rev er ent	in cor po rate	ar tis ti cal

LESSON LXXXII.

THE EARTH.

How goodly is the earth!
Its mountain tops behold
Its rivers broad and strong,
Its solemn forests old;
Behold the radiant isles,
With which the ocean smiles;
Behold the seasons run,
Obedient to the sun;
The gracious showers descend—
Life springing without end;
Behold all these, and know
How goodly is the earth.

How goodly is the earth!
Yet if the earth be made
So goodly, wherein all

That is shall droop and fade;
So goodly, where is strife
Ever 'twixt death and life;
Where trouble dims the eye,
Where sin hath mastery;
How much more bright and fair
Will be that region where
The saints of God shall rest,
Rejoicing, with the blest;
Where pain is not, nor death—
"The Paradise of God!"

THE HUMBLE AND CONTRITE.

For thus saith the high and lofty One that inhabiteth eternity, whose name is holy: I dwell in the high and holy place, with him also that is of a contrite and humble spirit, to revive the spirit of the humble, and to revive the heart of the contrite ones. Heaven is my throne, and the earth is my footstool; but to this man will I look, even to him that is poor and of a contrite spirit, and trembleth at my word.—*Bible.*

Words of Four Syllables, Accented on the Second.

ac cip i ent	de nom i nate	in firm a ry
ab dom i nal	pre var i cate	ad ven tu rous
ab sur di ty	an ni hi late	af firm a tive
ac com mo date	am mo ni ac	ap par i tor
al lo di um	am bil o quy	ex ec u tive
fa ce tious ly	am big u ous	ec cen tri cal
fer men ta tive	ad ver bi al	cen trip e tal
ap pro pri ate	am bas sa dor	cen trif u gal
se ver i ty	an nu i tant	con sol i date
so lid i ty	an tag o nist	he ro ic al
a per i tive	a nom a lous	hu mid i ty
fe roc i ty	an thol o gy	pa ter ni ty
flu id i ty	an tip o dal	fer ment a ble
a pos tro phe	an tip o des	fes tiv i ty
ap pa rent ly	an tiph o ny	fer til i ty
an ti ci pate	a poc a lypse	flu id i ty
dis cov er y	ap prox i mate	neu tral i ty

E*

LESSON LXXXIII.
PRAISE.

I'll praise my Maker with my breath,
And when my voice is lost in death,
  Praise shall employ my nobler powers;
My days of praise shall ne'er be past,
While life and thought and being last,
  Or immortality endures.

Happy the man whose hopes rely
On Israel's God; He made the sky,
  And earth and seas, with all their train:
His truth forever stands secure;
He saves the oppressed, He feeds the poor,
  And none shall find his promise vain.

He knows His saints, He loves them well,
But turns the wicked down to hell:
  Thy God, O Zion, ever reigns;
Let every tongue, let every age,
In this exalted work engage;
  Praise Him in everlasting strains.

Various Monosyllables.

sweat	cheese	helm	crawl
threat	squeeze	whelm	drawl
scheme	eight	fitch	switch
theme	weight	pitch	twitch
built	surge	snore	clink
guilt	purge	swore	think
tempt	brief	furl	cheat
dreamt	thief	churl	wheat
splint	cease	bourne	flounce
squint	lease	mourn	trounce
ounce	snout	drink	didst
pounce	spout	chink	midst

GOOD FOR EVIL.

1. Injustice, private injuries and a spirit of retaliation or revenge are the prolific sources of most evils found in human society.

2. Hence, as a most wise and beneficent provision, the rendering of evil for evil is divinely forbidden. "Recompense to no man evil for evil" is the divine command; and it is binding upon all men.

3. Another injunction is: "Be kindly affectioned, one to another, with brotherly love; in honor preferring one another." Again it is enjoined: "Bless them that curse you; bless, and curse not. If it be possible, as much as lieth in you, live peaceably with all men."

4. "Avenge not yourselves; but rather give place unto wrath; for it is written, Vengeance is mine. I will repay, saith the Lord."

5. "Therefore, if thine enemy hunger, feed him; if he thirst, give him drink; for, in so doing, thou shalt heap coals of fire on his head." "Be not overcome of evil, but overcome evil with good."

6. The known fact also is, that all men wish others to treat them justly, kindly and charitably. But the sum of the whole moral law is: "Whatsoever ye would that men should do unto you, do ye even so to them."

7. If all persons would observe this simple and beautiful rule, what a peaceful and happy world would we soon have, instead of its being full of contention, strife, evil speaking, war and bloodshed, as it has always been! Let all learn, then, to do as they would be done by.

LESSON LXXXIV.

SUBLIME THOUGHT.

Above the crowd,
On upward wings, could I but fly,
I'd bathe in yon bright cloud,
And seek the stars that gem the sky.

'Twere heaven indeed,
Through fields of trackless light to soar,
On nature's charms to feed,
And nature's own great God adore.

THE ZEBRA.

The little readers of this book would be greatly delighted to see the Zebra. It is found only in the interior of Africa, and is one of the wildest animals found on the globe. Few of them have ever been taken.

It is a very beautiful animal. Its form is very much like that of the horse, except that it is much smaller. Its body is round, compact and fleshy; its limbs slender and handsome. Its hair is smooth and glossy. It is destitute of mane, and has only a tuft of long hair on the end of its tail.

The whole body of the Zebra is covered with black and white stripes, which give it a very singular appearance. When in the forests and deserts, they are always on the watch; and their swiftness is such that it is exceedingly difficult to take them alive. In disposition, they are very vicious. To handle them is dangerous, to tame them scarcely possible.

So you see, children, that it is not every thing *beautiful* that is good or useful; and so long as you get nice little ponies, you need not desire this strange animal.

con tem pla tive	de clar a tive	dis cour te sy
con tempt i ble	de cli na ble	dis pen sa ry
con tempt u ous	de crep i tude	dis pla cen cy
con ter min ous	de cum ben cy	dis qual i fy
con test a ble	de ri va ble	dis qui e tude
con tig u ous	de struc ti ble	dog mat i cal
con trac ti ble	de light ful ly	ex tat i cal
con trib u tor	de mo ni ac	ef fec tu al
con vex i ty	de pop u late	ef fem i nate
co op er ate	di lu ci date	ef fron te ry
co or di nate	dis cern i ble	e lec tri cal
co part ner ship	dis ci ple ship	e lu ci date
cor po re al	dis con so late	e man ci pate
cor rob or ant	dis cour age ment	en bar rass ment
cru cif er ous	dis cov er y	em bel lish ment

LESSON LXXXV.

FEAR NO EVIL.

I need not fear an evil day,
While to my Heavenly King I pray;
For all my wants will be supplied
By Him who is my shield and guide.

I cannot in my Bible find
One word of *Fortune* being *kind;*
But this I know that Jesus came
To save me from eternal flame.

I know that unto Him is given
Almighty power in earth and heaven;
I know no other God can be,
Than He who showed such love for me.

Let but His blessing crown my store,
I need not look to *chance* for more,
Or let Him take my wealth away,
I yet will trust Him tho' He slay.

I ask but to be made His own,
I tremble at His wrath alone;
If I have grace His will to do,
I must be safe and happy too.

ART OF HAPPINESS.

A good temper and a cheerful disposition are the principal ingredients of happiness. Almost every object has its bright and its dark side. He that habitually looks upon the unpleasant side will sour his temper and impair his happiness. On the contrary, he that looks upon the side which is bright and pleasing will improve his temper, increase his happiness, and become a channel of communication by which the cheerfulness and enjoyment of all those around him will be enhanced.

Words of Two Syllables, Accented on the First.

In this and the following lists of words, *tion, cion* and *sion* are pronounced as if written "*shun:*"

ac tion	men tion	po tion	mix tion
dic tion	cau tion	sec tion	fric tion
ces sion	mis sion	sta tion	stric tion
fac tion	na tion	suc tion	sanc tion
fic tion	no tion	ten tion	spon sion
fu sion	pas sion	tor tion	auc tion
junc tion	pen sion	op tion	ses sion
lo tion	por tion	frac tion	fluc tion
man sion	mo tion	func tion	vis ion

LESSON LXXXVI.

DEPARTED FRIENDS.

Friend after friend departs;
  Who has not lost a friend?
There is no union here of hearts,
  That finds not here an end,
Were this frail world our final rest,
Living or dying, none were blest.

Beyond the flight of time,
  Beyond the reign of death,
There surely is some blessed clime,
  Where life is not a breath—
Nor life's affections transient fire,
Whose sparks fly upward and expire.

There is a world above,
  Where parting is unknown;
A long eternity of love,
  Formed for the good alone;
And faith beholds the dying here,
Translated to that glorious sphere.

Thus star by star declines,
  Till all are pass'd away,
A morning high and higher shines,
  To pure and perfect day;
Nor sink those stars in empty night,
But hide themselves in heaven's own light.

Words of Three Syllables, Accented on the Second. Their terminations are pronounced as if written SHUN *or* ZHUN.

ab ra sion	al lu sion	in spec tion
ac ces sion	co he sion	con cep tion
ab lu tion	col la tion	cor rup tion
ad di tion	fru i tion	de struc tion
ad dic tion	ig ni tion	in struc tion
af flic tion	il lu sion	pro fu sion
af fu sion	in fu sion	pro pul sion

cog ni tion	in fec tion	re vul sion
de cis ion	in flic tion	sub ver sion
di vis ion	im mer sion	sub mer sion
de tru sion	in jec tion	re ver sion
col lis ion	in junc tion	pre emp tion
com mis sion	in tru sion	re demp tion
com mo tion	in va sion	se ces sion
con di tion	oc ca sion	con fes sion
co ac tion	ob la tion	cor rec tion
co emp tion	at ten tion	e vic tion
com ple tion	con ten tion	e mis sion
com pul sion	sal va tion	re mis sion
com pres sion	pro vis ion	per mis sion
de vo tion	re vis ion	pro duc tion
dis plo sion	in cis ion	pre dic tion
dis cus sion	in va sion	col lec tion
de lu sion	per va sion	con fec tion
af fec tion	per sua sion	in fec tion
e lec tion	pre ven tion	in spec tion
as cen sion	con ten tion	pre lec tion
as per sion	cre a tion	in ven tion
at ten tion	pri va tion	sus pi cion
dis per sion	vo ca tion	im mis sion
con cis ion	ro ga tion	in cis ion
co er cion	suf fu sion	di vis ion
ad he sion	suc ces sion	de flec tion
dis mis sion	sus pen sion	du ra tion

LESSON LXXXVII.

ANECDOTES.

BECLOUDED.

A sprightly gentleman, whose name was *Fowler*, married a Miss *Cloud*. A friend, congratulating him on the occasion, expressed the hope that, though he had for several months been quite "*beclouded*," he would now have bright sunshine before him the rest of his days. Another friend replied: "That is hoping against hope; for the well known adage is, 'When clouds turn, *'fowler*,' look out for *squalls*.'"

LAUGHING.

A gentleman walking along the street saw another person look that way and laugh. Feeling indignant, he, with much warmth, enquired: "Why do you laugh as I pass by?" The other promptly retorted: "Why do you pass by as I laugh?"

The terminations TIAN *and* TION, *in the following words, are pronounced as if written* CHUN:

chris tian	ad us tion	con ges tion
fus tian	di ges tion	ad mix tion
bas tion	com bus tion	ex haus tion
mix tion	ex us tion	sug ges tion
ques tion	in ges tion	in di ges tion

The terminations in the following words are pronounced like ZHUN:

di vis ion	pro vis ion	in cis ion
pre cis ion	e lis ion	de ris ion
de cis ion	col lis ion	ab scis ion
re vis ion	re scis ion	con cis ion
ex cis ion	mis pris ion	pre vis ion

In spelling the following words ending in IC, *the syllable* AL *should be added to each of them, and then* LY *to that:* Critic, critical, critically:

con ic	clin ic	crit ic	cu bic
cyn ic	log ic	eth ic	eth nic
clas sic	caus tic	cen tric	com ic
lyr ic	mys tic	mu sic	mag ic
skep tic	op tic	phthis ic	spher ic
stat ic	sto ic	styp tic	top ic
rus tic	graph ic	typ ic	trag ic

Words of Three Syllables in TION, *Accented on the Second.*

sub trac tion	re jec tion	re ten tion
dis trac tion	sub jec tion	ex ten sion
se lec tion	se lec tion	ex pul sion
dis sec tion	re gres sion	ex pan sion

ci ta tion	di gres sion	ex er tion
vi bra tion	gy ra tion	cau sa tion
stag na tion	pol lu tion	car na tion
gra da tion	de mis sion	per sua sion
dam na tion	de ser tion	in tru sion
pros tra tion	con ver sion	ro ta tion
pul sa tion	con vic tion	sen sa tion
mi gra tion	cor rep tion	dis mis sion
li ba tion	de duc tion	e mul sion
pro ba tion	dis cur sion	an tla tion
ces sa tion	de tec tion	cor ro sion
plan ta tion	pro tec tion	tax a tion
po ta tion	pre ten sion	quo ta tion
so lu tion	pri va tion	vex a tion
o va tion	ex cus sion	sa na tion
lu na tion	ex trac tion	re func tion
lux a tion	ex plo sion	ex cre tion

LESSON LXXXVIII.

THE WASP AND THE BEE.

A wasp met a bee that was just buzzing by,
And he said: little cousin, can you tell me why
You are loved so much better by people than I?

My back shines as bright and as yellow as gold,
And my shape is most elegant, too, to behold;
Yet no body likes me for that, I am told.

"Ah, friend," said the bee, "that is all very true,
But were I half as much mischief to do,
Then people would love me no better than you.

"You have a fine shape, and a delicate wing,
You are perfectly handsome, but then there's one thing
They can never put up with, and that is your sting.

"My coat is quite homely and plain, as you see,
Yet no body ever is angry with me,
Because I'm a useful and innocent bee."

From this little lesson let people beware;
For if, like the wasp, they ill-natured are,
They will never be loved, tho' they're ever so fair.

In the following lists of words, *ce, ci, ti* and *si* have the sound of SH:

Words of Two Syllables, Accented on the First.

gra cious	vi tiate	so cial
con science	pre cious	gen tian
spa cious	par tial	Gre cian
fac tious	an cient	cau tious
lus cious	ques tion	vi cious
spe cious	cap tious	spe cial
ter tian	mar tial	nup tial
frac tious	spe cies	pa tient
con scious	fic tious	quo tient

Words of Three Syllables, Accented on the Second.

as so ciate	an nun ciate	in gra tiate
dis so ciate	no vi tiate	in sa tiate
ne go tiate	e ma ciate	sub stan tiate
ex cru ciate	con so ciate	of fi ciate

Words of Three Syllables, ending in TIOUS *and* CIOUS, *Accented on the Second.*

a tro cious	am bi tious	se qua cious
au da cious	aus pi cious	vi va cious
fal la cious	nu tri tious	vo ra cious
pre co cious	fla gi tious	con ten tious
sa ga cious	ma li cious	li cen tious
fe ro cious	pro pi tious	in cau tious
te na cious	ca pa cious	de li cious
vex a tious	fa ce tious	of fi cious
crus ta cious	lo qua cious	sus pi cious
in fec tious	ra pa cious	per ni cious
sen ten tious	ve ra cious	se di tious

LESSON LXXXIX.

THAT LAZY BOY!

1. That lazy lad! and what's his name?
   I would not like to tell;
   But don't you think it is a shame
   That he can't read or spell?

2. He'd rather swing upon a gate,
 Or paddle in a brook,
Than take his pencil and his slate,
 Or try to read his book.

3. There, see! he's lounging down the street,
 His hat without a rim;
He'd rather drag than lift his feet—
 His face unwashed and grim.

4. He's lolling now against a post,
 But if you've seen him once,
You'll know the lad among a host,
 For what he is—a *dunce*.

5. Don't ask me what's the urchin's name,
 I do not choose to tell;
But this you'll know—it is the same
As his who does not blush for shame,
 That he don't read or spell!

"I'll let you down easy this time," as the horse said when he upset his master in the deep bog.

"If you beat me I'll call out the soldiery," said the drum.

"This is the day we celebrate," said the fat turkies to each other, on a bright Christmas morning.

Words of Four Syllables, Accented on the Third.

cal c fac tion	im pli ca tion	en er va tion
bal ne a tion	sup pli ca tion	em u la tion
cal ci na tion	rep li ca tion	am pu ta tion
cap i ta tion	vac il la tion	ap pli ca tion
cir cum cis ion	mac er a tion	an i ma tion
cir cum spec tion	sal i va tion	nav i ga tion
cog i ta tion	nav i ga tion	ob li ga tion
col li qua tion	pec u la tion	cor ru ga tion
com bi na tion	rad i ca tion	im pre ca tion
com men da tion	prov o ca tion	im pu ta tion
com mu ta tion	stim u la tion	ju di ca tion
com pen sa tion	stip u la tion	al lo cu tion

con ca va tion	rev e la tion	com men da tion
con clam a tion	el o cu tion	con se cra tion
con for ma tion	el e va tion	cor o na tion
con glo ba tion	em bar ca tion	ex pe di tion
con tra ven tion	ex til la tion	com pe ti tion
con ver sa tion	ex su da tion	con firm a tion
con vo lu tion	ex ul ta tion	com pli ca tion
con vo ca tion	fab ri ca tion	dem o li tion
cor o na tion	fec un da tion	des ig na tion
cor rus ca tion	fer men ta tion	ag i ta tion
dec la ra tion	fil i a tion	lam en ta tion
dec la ma tion	em u la tion	mac u la tion
dec o ra tion	ed u ca tion	lac er a tion
ded i ca tion	eb ul li tion	mas ti ca tion
dem on stra tion	ex ei ta tion	nav i ga tion
dep o si tion	flag el la tion	prop a ga tion
der i va tion	fluc tu a tion	com pu ta tion
des ti tu tion	bi fur ca tion	con cen tra tion
dis qui si tion	cu mu la tion	con ster na tion
dis ser ta tion	cir cu la tion	ad ju ra tion
dis si pa tion	ded i ca tion	ad ju va tion
dom i na tion	del e ga tion	in flam ma tion
du pli ca tion	e lon ga tion	

LESSON XC.

SAYINGS.

Dr. South says the author of a malevolent slander, and the person who listens to it, are equally guilty, and should both be hung; but with this difference—the one by the tongue, the other by the ear.

No one can say, I will sin just so far and no farther. Sin is like a snow ball rolling down a hill—small at first, but increasing as it goes, till it becomes an overwhelming mountain.

Punch says that "Time is money;" but it does not follow that a man is a very heavy capitalist who has a great deal of it on hand.

The worst of all feuds, collisions and heart burnings are those which pertain to the domestic circle. Those who value peace, comfort and enjoyment should avoid them as they would death. As a preventive, *honey* is the best prescription. *Vinegar is deadly.*

Words of Four Syllables, ending in tion, Accented on the Third.

ac cep ta tion	ab so lu tion	ex plo ra tion
ad ap ta tion	af fir ma tion	ex tir pa tion
ac cla ma tion	an no ta tion	ex ul ta tion
ac cu ba tion	ag gra va tion	ex pli ca tion
a cer va tion	em en da tion	ex po si tion
am bu la tion	in car na tion	ex cla ma tion
am pu ta tion	en er va tion	ex an tla tion
am mu ni tion	ex pi ra tion	ex ce la tion
an i ma tion	ex cla ma tion	ex hi bi tion
an nex a tion	ev o la tion	ex hor ta tion
ap pa ri tion	em u la tion	ex su da tion
ap pel la tion	ev o lu tion	im mo la tion
ap pe ti tion	ev o mi tion	im per fec tion
ap pli ca tion	ex al ta tion	im pli ca tion
ap po si tion	ex e cra tion	im por ta tion
ap pre hen sion	ex pe di tion	im po si tion
ap pro ba tion	ex pla na tion	im pre ca tion
ab ju ra tion	ex por ta tion	im preg na tion
ab ne ga tion	ex po si tion	in can ta tion
ab o li tion	ex pur ga tion	in car na tion

LESSON XCI.

A CONTRAST.

Some murmur when their sky is clear,
   And wholly bright to view,
If one small speck of dark appear
   In their great heaven of blue;
And some with thankful love are filled,
   If but one streak of light,
One ray of God's good mercy, gild
   The darkness of their night.

> In palaces are hearts that ask,
> In discontent and pride,
> Why life is such a dreary task,
> And all good things denied;
> And hearts in poorest huts admire
> How love has, in their aid,
> (Love that not even seems to tire,)
> Such rich provision made.—*Trench.*

In the following words "sion" are pronounced ZHUN, *and "sia" like* ZHA:

af fu sion	co he sion	de lu sion
ad he sion	e va sion	e ro sion
ef fu sion	ex plo sion	pro fu sion
a bra sion	col lu sion	dis plo sion
dif fu sion	e lu sion	per va sion
oc ca sion	con clu sion	cor ro sion
con fu sion	il lu sion	in va sion
in tru sion	in va sion	suf fu sion
ob tru sion	dis sua sion	e ro sion
per sua sion	de tru sion	pro tru sion
am bro sia	am bro sial	se clu sion
col lu sion	dif fu sion	ex clu sion

A FABLE.

THE OWL AND THE EAGLE.

An owl that had often heard of the keenness and strength of the eagle's eye sight, bantered that lord of the feathered tribes to swap eyes with her. "Mine," said she, "are larger than yours, and they are better also, for you can see with them in the night."

"I decline the trade," said the eagle. "Your nature leads you to seek your prey in the night; mine, in the clear sunshine. A change of eyes would impel to a change both of nature and of occupation; and that might prove fatal to us both."

MORAL.

Discontent and a restless anxiety for change of condition or occupation, are the enemies both of enjoyment and life.

CONUNDRUM.

Why was Frederick, when leaving home on a journey for the recovery of his health, like a man who had fallen from a tree, and was determined to go up again? Because he was going to try another *clime*.

Prentice says: "It is bad *husbandry* when a man harrows up his wife's feelings."

LESSON XCII.

THE ROBIN.

PURE COLD WATER.

I asked a sweet robin, one morning in May,
Who sang in the apple tree over the way,
What 'twas she was singing so sweetly about,
For I'd tried a long time, but could not find out;
"Why I'm," she replied, "you cannot guess wrong,
Don't you know I'm singing a *temperance song?*"

"Teetotal."—O, that's the first word of the lay,
And then don't you see how I twitter about;
'Tis because I've just dipped my beak in the spring,
And brushed the fair face of the lake with my wing;
"Cold water, cold water," yes, that is my song,
And I love to keep singing it all the day long.

And now, my sweet Miss, won't you give me a crumb,
For the dear little nestlings are waiting at home?
And one thing besides, since my story you've heard,
I hope you'll remember "the lay of the bird;"
And never forget while you list to my song,
All the *birds* to the cold water army belong."

Hood's Melodies.

In the following words of two syllables, accented on the first, the *u* of the last syllable has the sound of *yu*, or is preceded by the sound of *y*:

na ture	mix ture	pic ture	sculp ture
tor ture	fea ture	pos ture	Scrip ture
su ture	cap ture	lec ture	rup ture
stric ture	tex ture	join ture	punc ture
nur ture	stat ure	ves ture	mois ture
rap ture	struc ture	tinc ture	junc ture

G and k are always silent before *n*. The following words illustrate that fact:

gnarl	kneel	gno mon	knit ting
gnash	know	gnos tics	knight hood
gnar	knew	knap sack	knav ish
gnat	knife	knap weed	knuc kle
gnaw	knight	knock er	knot ted
knob	knit	knock ing	kna ver y
knock	knob	knot ty	kna vish ly
knap	knock	knot grass	knight er rant
knave	knoll	knot less	knot ti ly
knur	knot	know ing	knot ti ness
knead	knout	know er	know ing ly
knee	knurl	knowl edge	know a ble

LESSON XCIII.

BIRDS.

A light broke in upon my soul—
It was the carol of a bird;
It ceased and then it came again,
The sweetest song ear ever heard.

THE HOOPOO.

Children are fond of birds. I wish they could all see the one I am about to describe. But it is not found in this country. The hoopoo is quite a pretty and quite an innocent bird. It is nearly twelve inches long, and is about the size of a pigeon. Its bill is long and slender, and it curves gently toward its breast. It is of a red color about its head and neck, but it has bars of white and black across its wings. It has a crest of feathers on its head, which fall back upon its neck; but when it becomes excited, they rise in the form of a half circle above its head.

Its tail consists of ten-feathers, several inches long, and they are so arranged that when it is closed it forms a narrow fan in shape at the end like the new moon—the longest feathers being at the edges.

The hoopoo belongs to Europe, but it goes to warmer

climates in the winter. It never makes a nest, but hides its eggs in holes or crevices of the walls of houses or other buildings. Take it all together it is a rare bird, and it is here described because it is so singular.

In the following words *ng* are heard, sharp and close, in both syllables:

clan gor	an ger	an gle
dan gle	an gry	an gler
an guish	con go	din gle
fan gle	din gle	fun gus
fin ger	hun gry	in gle
hun ger	jan gler	jan gling
jun gle	lan guid	lan guish
jin gle	long est	man go
lon ger	min gle	man gler
sin gle	strong est	young est

THE RAINBOW is caused by the sun's rays passing through drops of water. The rays are thus divided into the seven different colors; and these, meeting the eye at a certain angle as they are thrown off from the countless drops that fall during a shower, form that beautiful, many-colored arch.

LESSON XCIV.

MORNING SONG OF GLADNESS.

As a bird in meadow fair,
  Or in lonely forest sings,
Till it fills the summer air,
  And the greenwood sweetly rings;

So my heart to Thee would raise,
Oh! my God, its song of praise,
That the gloom of night is o'er,
And I see the sun once more.

If thou, Sun of Love, arise,
  All my heart with joy is stirred,
And to greet Thee upward flies,
  Gladsome as yon little bird.

F

Shine thou in me clear and bright,
Till I learn to praise Thee right;
Guide me in the narrow way,
Let me ne'er in darkness stray.

By Thy spirit strengthen me,
In the faith that leads to Thee,
Then an heir of life on high,
Fearless I may live and die.

G is silent in the following words:

sign	re sign	de sign	im pregn
as sign	con dign	ma lign	in dign
con sign	be nign	im pugn	en sign

The vowels in the second syllable of the following words are mute:

ba con	bea con	bra zen
hid den	bid den	box en
black en	boun den	but ton
bat ten	beech en	ba sin
bla zon	beat en	bit ten
cho sen	beck on	clo ven

Words of two syllables, in which *th* have the soft or vocal sound:

fath er	breth ren	lath er	with er
feath er	whith er	far thing	heath en
fath om	cloth ier	ei ther	South ern
gath er	North ern	nei ther	un wreathe
lath er	broth er	thith er	be neath
poth er	moth er	leath er	be queath
broth el	wor thy	oth er	weath er

LESSON XCV.

THE LAW AND THE GOSPEL.

There is a God who reigns above,
  Lord of heaven, and earth, and seas;
I fear his wrath, I ask his love,
  And with my lips I sing his praise.

There is a law which He has writ,
  To teach us all that we must do;
My soul to His commands submit,
  For they are holy, just and true.

There is a gospel of rich grace,
  Whence sinners all their comforts draw;
Lord, I repent and seek Thy face,
  For I have often broke Thy law.

There is an hour when I must die,
  Nor do I know how soon 'twill come;
A thousand children, young as I,
  Are called to their eternal home.

Let me improve the hours I have,
  Before the day of grace is fled;
For there's no repentance in the grave,
  Nor pardon offered to the dead.

SOURCE OF COLORS.

The lovely colors, light and shade,
  Of every varied hue,
All these our heavenly Father made,
  All praise to Him is due.

A colorless world, what would it be! Light is the source of all color. Had light been made different from what it is, there would either have been no color, or the colors would have been different from those which we now see.

Were there no light, perfect blackness would cover the whole face of nature. Light, as it comes to us from the sun, is *white*. But when divided, it is found to consist of seven different colors. These are called red, orange, yellow, green, blue, indigo, violet.

Now, the reason why bodies have so many different appearances as regards color is this: Bodies that absorb all the light which falls on them are *black*, just as all the world would be if there were no light. Others that reflect all the rays are *white*. They do not divide the light at all. The black bodies swallow it whole; the white ones throw it back whole. The light comes to our eyes from them just as it was before it fell upon them. That is the reason why they appear *white*. All other bodies divide the light, absorb most of the rays, but throw back some of them. The body that appears red throws off the red rays. The blue body throws back the blue rays. And so of all the rest. By this simple, and yet wonderful process, all the different colors are produced! Truly God's ways of doing things are calculated to fill us with wonder and delight. Try now whether, when you look at different objects, you can tell what each one does with the light that falls upon it. Remember that each body appears to be of the same color with the light it reflects.

LESSON XCVI.

THE RAINBOW.

Far up the blue sky a fair rainbow unrolled
Its soft-tinted pinions of purple and gold;
'Twas born in a moment, yet quick at its birth,
It had stretched to the uttermost ends of the earth;
And fair as an angel, it floated as free,
With a wing on the earth and a wing on the sea.

I in the beginning of a syllable, in the following words, has the sound of the consonant *y;* bill-ion is pronounced as if written *bill-yon*, and so in all the other words:

Sav iour	min ion	brill iant	dis un ion
court ier	pin ion	bat tal ion	pe cul iar
pav ior	trill ion	pa vil ion	be hav ior
jun ion	pon iard	fa mil iar	ci vil ian
cloth ier	val iant	ver mil ion	se ragl io
sen ior	on ion	com mun ion	al ien ate
bill ion	bill iards	mo dill ion	val iant ly
coll ier	scull ion	com pan ion	bil ia ry
fil ial	runn ion	o pin ion	brill ian cy
mill ion	trunn ion	re bell ion	val iant ness

ANECDOTES.

THE SCOTCHMEN.

Two elderly Scotchmen, full of dry humor, were spending an evening together. One of them complained of a *ringing* in his head. The other promptly and earnestly enquired: "Do you know why it rings?" "No," said his afflicted companion, "I do not." "Then," said he, "I will tell you; it is because it is *empty!*"

"And do you never have a ringing in your head," enquired "empty" head of the other. "No, *never*," said he. "And do you know why that is?" "No," said he. "Well, then, I will tell you," said the other. "It is because it is *cracked!*"

CLEOPATRA'S decoction of diamonds, as a rare dish, was fairly exceeded in originality and neatness of conception by the English sailor, who placed a ten pound note between two slices of bread and butter, and made his black-eyed Susan eat it as a sandwich.

LESSON XCVII.

THE SLOTHFUL.

As vinegar to the teeth, and as smoke to the eyes, so is the sluggard to them that send him.

Epaminondas, the Theban General, having found a sentinel asleep at his post, thrust him thro' with his sword and left him dead! When others cast up that act to him as a reproach, he replied: "*I left him as I found him!*" His meaning was that idlers, drones and sluggards are at once *dead* to all the ends of their being, and as useless to the world as dead people are.

Man was made for activity and enterprise. Our first parents were placed in a magnificent garden—an inviting field of action—and they were required to "*dress it and keep it.*" Alas! that any of their descendants should ever become "creation's blank, creation's blot."

Would we fill our stations aright, we must be at once *good, active* and *useful.*

In this list of words c, s and t have the sound of sh when followed by i or u: ra-ti-o, ra-shc-o:

cen sure	ton sure	pre science	pre sci ent
fis sure	tis sue	spa ci ate	pre sci ous
is sue	as sure	sa ti ate	gra ci ate
pres sure	en sure	ra ti o	gla ci al
spe cies	in sure	gla ci ate	cas si a
in su lar	com men su rate	men su ra tion	
con su lar	fi du ci a ry	con so ci ate	
sen su al	an nun ci ate	in sa ti a ble	
as su rance	dis so ci ate	of fi ci ate	
li cen ti ate	in gra ti ate	ex pa ti ate	
pro pi ti ate	ne go ti a tor	ne go ti ate	
e ma ci ate	con so ci a tion	e nun ci ate	
vi ti a tion	e nun ci a tion	as so ci a tion	
ap pre ci ate	pro pi ti a tion	an nun ci a tion	

Regard every day of your life as a page of your history. Be careful, therefore, that nothing be written on it which, at last, you would wish to have blotted out. Once entered, the record is made forever.

LESSON XCVIII.

FRUITS.

FRUITS stand prominent among our earthly blessings. They add, at once, to substantial living and grateful enjoyment. They come early, pour forth their summer abundance, and not a few of them abide with us through the winter. What warm friends, what welcome visitors are they on cold winter evenings!

The only wonder is, that through our whole Confederacy, they have not been multiplied a thousand fold! Roll on, blessed day, when they shall cluster round the dwellings of the poor, adorn the grounds and load the tables of all our substantial planters, and fill, with their profusion of luxuries the cellars of the wealthy and the great, of whatever profession or calling.

Men are public benefactors who introduce into our

country fine varieties, and supply their fellow-citizens with grafted vines and trees of the most approved qualities.

The South is the land of fruits as well as of flowers. Taking our whole Confederacy together, we can raise more kinds of fruits, and most of them better ones, than can be reared in the States farther North.

Trees once procured, it requires but little labor to keep them in order. No yearly planting is required as in other crops. All the attention they require affords but a delightful occupation for leisure hours. FRUITS, FRUITS! let them, then, be everywhere found, everywhere enjoyed.

Words of Five Syllables, Accented on the Third.

cir cum an bi ent	in de scri ba ble	sub ter ra ne ous
cir cum lo cu tion	an i mal i ty	cir cu la to ry
cir cum vo lu tion	in car nal i ty	in ad ver tent ly
op por tu ni ty	in ex cu sa ble	mis cel la ne ous
im por tu ni ty	in com pat i ble	mi cros cop i cal
an ni ver sa ry	mag is te ri al	cos mo graph i cal
im me mo ri al	lit er a ri an	hy dro stat i cal
im ma te ri al	mat ri mo ni al	an a tom i cal
un con ge ni al	sen a to ri al	as tro nom i cal
un ad vi sed ly	min is te ri al	in tro duc to ry
det ri men tal ly	dic ta to ri al	in ter ja cen cy
dis in gen u ous	in se cu ri ty	suc ce da ne ous
in con so la ble	in de struc ti ble	par si mo ni ous
ir re spon si ble	in tel lec tu al	pen i ten tia ry
an ti mo ni al	in ef fi cien cy	per son al i ty
in ter cal a ry	in co he rent ly	pop u lar i ty
in ac ces si ble	par lia ment a ry	pos si bil i ty
in ad ver ten cy	pat ri mo ni al	prob a bil i ty
tes ta men ta ry	mer i to ri ous	prod i gal i ty
tel e graph i cal	si mul ta ne ous	in si pid i ty

LESSON XCIX.
STAND FOR THE RIGHT.

Be firm, be bold, be strong, be true,
And dare to stand alone;
Strive for the right, whate'er ye do,
Though helpers there are none.

Nay, bend not to the swelling surge
  Of public sneer and wrong;
'Twill bear thee on to ruin's verge,
  With current wild and strong.

Stand for the right! tho' falsehood rail,
  And proud lips coldly sneer—
A poisoned arrow cannot wound
  A conscience pure and clear,

Stand for the right! and with clean hands
  Exalt the truth on high;
Thou'lt find warm, sympathizing hearts
  Among the passers-by.

Stand for the right! proclaim it loud,
  Thou'lt find an answering tone
In honest hearts, and thou'lt no more
  Be doomed to stand alone.

TOO INQUISITIVE AND MISCHIEVOUS.

A FABLE.

A monkey saw his master hide something in his garden. He marked the place with his eye, and, when he thought no one saw him, he went and raked away the covering to see what had been so carefully concealed. But instead of discovering a treasure, suddenly he found his paw caught in a trap, by which he was maimed for the rest of his life.

MORAL.

Never meddle with that which neither belongs to you, nor concerns you.

Words of Four Syllables, Accented on the Second.

a bom i nate	im per fect ly	mi rac u lous
a nat o my	per fid i ous	im per ti nent
a nal o gous	fas tid i ous	im per son al
a non y mous	u nan i mous	im pla ca ble
bar bar i ty	un gen er ous	im pos si ble
be nev o lent	as par a gus	mu nif i cent
am big u ous	pre cip it ous	im prov i dent
ca day er ous	am phib i ous	non res i dent

ca lum ni ate	in gen u ous	be nef i cent
fruc tif er ous	in con gru ous	pre dom i nant
im mis ci ble	sig nif i cant	ex trav a gant
im ped i ment	con com i tant	ha bil i ment
im pa tient ly	mag nif i cent	im ped i ment
im pen i tent	co in ci dent	im pet u ous
im per a tive	in dem ni fy	

LESSON C.

MAN.

Scarce less, at first, than angels made,
And then for him that ransom paid!
How majestic, god-like and grand,
When all his noblest powers expand!

ERECT POSITION.

It is the glory of man, that while the brute creation are prone—inclining to the earth—his Maker gave to him an erect position and a lofty countenance. Nor is the "human face divine" more worthy of admiration than the agile movements of the human frame, when its symmetry is complete and every muscle plays well its part.

And yet where can we look upon a crowd of human beings, without being pained at beholding the curved spines, the rounded shoulders, the sunken chests, the projecting necks, the rigid muscles, and the awkward and slovenly movements of many a lord or lady of this lower creation!

The origin of most of these deformities, and the causes of these painful sights, are found in the shameful neglect of *physical training* in our family circles and our institutions of learning.

An erect position, with the chest expanded, the countenance slightly elevated, and the weight of the body thus supported at ease over the feet, is at once the most *healthful* as well as the most *dignified* and *graceful* that can be occupied. And yet, with a little attention to training, in early life, how easily is this acquired and retained!

It should, therefore, be the law of every family and every school, *that children and youth stand erect, sit erect, walk erect*, and that every motor muscle be trained to easy and graceful movements. How different, and how vastly improved a race of beings, would we soon be were these simple laws of nature strictly enforced! Parents and teachers have before them, in this department, a wide field for beneficent effort.

BOASTING.

A Kentuckian once boasted that he could dive deeper, stay down longer, and come up *drier* than any other man on the globe.

LESSON CI.

INNOCENT PLAY.

Abroad in the meadows to see the young lambs
Run sporting about by the side of their dams,
With fleeces so clean and so white;
Or a nest of young doves, in a large open cage,
When they play all in love, without anger or rage,
How much may we learn from the sight!

If we had been ducks, we might dabble in mud;
Or dogs, we might play till it ended in blood,
So foul and so fierce are their natures;
But Thomas and William, and such pretty names,
Should be cleanly and harmless as doves or as lambs—
Those lovely, sweet, innocent creatures.

Not a thing that we do, not a word that we say,
Should injure another, in jesting or play,
For he's still in earnest that's hurt!
How rude are boys that throw pebbles and mire!
There's none but a madman will fling about fire,
And tell you " 'Tis all but in sport."

THE DOG AND THE SHADOW.

A FABLE.

A dog, with a large piece of flesh in his mouth, was crossing a smooth and limpid stream, on a clear sunny day. His shadow was so strongly depicted on the stream, that he took it for another dog equally laden with a similar booty. His eager desires got the better of his judgment. Letting go his own, he plunged at the meat of the supposed other dog! He grasped but a shadow! And, in the meantime, his own valued prize had sunk to the bottom.

MORAL.

Look before you leap. Never let go the substance to grasp at shadows.

A wasted morning makes a sad and dark evening.

If there be no sowing, there can be no gathering; but if no gathering, there must be extreme want and wretchedness.

Words of Five Syllables, Accented on the Second.

ac cept a ble ness	im me di ate ly	in cal cu la ble
ac com mo da ble	im med i ca ble	in can ta to ry
ac com mo date ly	il lib er al ly	men da ci ous ness
ac com pa na ble	il lim it a ble	me thod i cal ly
ac com pa ni ment	il lit er a cy	ju rid i cal ly
ac cus tom a ble	il lit er ate ness	un for tu nate ly
a nath e ma tize	im port u nate ly	in tol er a bly
a poth e ca ry	im pen e tra ble	in or di nate ly
ap pre ci a ble	im pe ri ous ly	un an swer a ble
a bol ish a ble	im pe ri ous ness	ir reg u lar ly
a bom i na ble	im per ish a ble	in tem per ate ly
ab ste mi ous ness	im prac ti ca ble	in sep a ra bly
fa mil i ar ize	im prov i dent ly	pre pos ter ous ly
fe lo ni ous ly	in ap pli ca ble	pre sump tu ous ly
im mod er ate ly	in a lien a ble	con sec u tive ly
im ag in a ble	in ap pe ten cy	con spic u ous ly

LESSON CII.

FEAR GOD.

Remember now thy Creator in the days of thy youth, while the evil days come not, nor the years draw nigh, when thou shalt say I have no pleasure in them.

Fear God and keep His commandments, for this is the whole duty of man.

WILD OATS.

We often hear it said of dissipated and reckless youth that "they are *sowing their wild oats,* and when they get through they will become sober, industrious, and valuable members of society." But when will they *"get through?"* Ah! there are many who "get through" very soon! A candle on fire at both ends is quickly burnt out. But suppose they should live to old age, what have they profited by their past course? An early life of indolence, dissipation and crime is the poorest of all qualifications for future enjoyment and usefulness. Besides, it is a fearful truth, that

>The seed of wild oats never dies,
>One growth having past ten others arise.

Each crop also produces its own peculiar fruit; and so will it be to the end. For "whatsoever a man soweth that shall he also reap." And that, too, with an *increase*, often, of many fold! For "they that sow the wind shall reap the whirlwind."

Let it, then, be borne in mind by every youth, that "wild oats" are the poorest crop that ever has been sowed, and the least satisfactory to *the owners* of all that ever have been gathered. And worst of all, they, in a short time, so deeply *impoverish* and *poison* the *soil*, that it seldom, if ever, produces anything valuable afterwards.

In this lesson, *e* when not silent, has the sound of *a* long. *Neigh, their* and *obey* are pronounced as if written nay, thare, obay:

obey	they	ere	o bey sance
co heir	there	tete	pur vey or
eigh ty	their	sley	sur vey ing
hein ous	tray	rein	con vey ance
neigh bor	skein	reign	dis o bey
par terre	vein	heir	there in to
in veigh	weigh	neigh	there un to
pur vey	whore	eight	there with al
sur vey	whey	freight	con nois seur

DAGGERS AND THORNS.

Many a reckless youth by a single thrust of his dagger plants a thousand thorns in his own pillow for the remainder of his life. Be guarded. Worlds offered as a price can never retrieve the deed, or restore your peace of mind.

LESSON CIII.

THE HEAVENS.

The shining worlds above
 In glorious order stand,
Or in swift courses move,
 By God's supreme command.
　- He spake the word,
　 And all their frame,
　 From nothing came.
　 To praise the Lord.

He moved their mighty wheels,
 In unknown ages past,
And earth His word fulfills,
 While time and nature last.
　 In different ways
　 His works proclaim
　 His wondrous-name,
　 And speak His praise.

G has two sounds—the hard and the soft. Its soft sound is like that of *j*. It is hard before *a*, *o* and *u*; but it is sometimes hard and sometimes soft before *e*, *i* and *y*. In the following lesson it is hard before these last named letters:

geese	fin ger	flag gy	stag ger
gear	lin ger	gid dy	swag ger
get	mon ger	gib bous	sprig gy
geld	mea ger	gim let	slug gish
gimp	ea ger	girl ish	snag gy
gild	ti ger	gig let	shag gy
give	big ger	gig gle	scrag ged
gig	bug gy	rig ger	twig ged
gird	mag gy	rig ging	twig gy
girl	sog gy	dig ger	trig ger
girth	bog gy	dig ging	leg gin
gift	nog gin	wag gish	bag ging
leg ged	tar get	wag ging	geld ing

rag ged	drug get	cog ger	gild ing
pig gin	drug gist	hug ged	gil der
an ger	flog ging	hug ging	gird er
au ger	flog ged	rug ged	gir dle
snag ged	shrug ged	tug ged	brag ger
gew gaw	shrug ging	log ged	brag ging
dog ged	gif ted	get ting	swag ging
dog gish	fog gy	fag ged	tag ging
hog gish	jag gy	jag ged	

Words in which *ch* have the sound of *sh;* and *i* that of *e* long:

chaise	cap a pie	cav a lier
chan cre	cap u chin	cor de lier
cham ade	car bin ier	man da rin
cham paign	can non ier	po lice
chi cane	brig a dier	ma rine
chev er il	bom ba zine	fas cine
chev a lier	sub ma rine	cash ier
chiv al ry	trans ma rine	fron tier
chan de lier	mag a zine	der nier

CURTIUS.

VALOR AND PATRIOTISM.

It is said that a fearful torrent, from beneath the surface, once burst up in the Forum of ancient Rome. The populace became alarmed. The Augurs were consulted. Their response was, that the breach never could be closed until the most precious things in Rome were thrown into it.

Upon hearing this, Curtius, a noble-minded and heroic Roman, clad in complete armor, and mounted on horseback, leaped into the midst of it, declaring that there was nothing more valuable than *valor* and *patriotism*.

The historians declare that the gulf immediately closed, and that Curtius was seen no more.

There is many a *moral breach* in this our beloved Confederacy, whose bitter and poisonous floods would overwhelm and desolate our whole land! Who and where are the self-sacrificing sons of the South that are ready, as the embodiment of valor and christian patriotism, to achieve immortal honor by a similar procedure?

LESSON CIV.

GOD'S PRAISE.

Let every creature join
  To praise the eternal God;
Ye heavenly hosts, the song begin,
  And sound His name abroad.

Thou sun with golden beams,
  And moon with paler rays,
Ye starry lights, ye twinkling flames,
  Shine to your Maker's praise.

He built those worlds above,
  And fixed their wondrous frame;
By his command they stand or move,
  And ever speak His name.

THE MOON.

This beautiful orb has no light of its own. It shines only by reflecting the light of the sun. That side of it which is turned toward the sun is bright; the other side is dark.

The moon is a small body, chiefly made to give light upon the earth. The distance through it is only two thousand miles. Its distance from the earth is two hundred and forty thousand miles. It completes its revolution round the earth, as its centre of motion, once in twenty-nine days and a half.

The appearances of the moon are very different in the different parts of its orbit. These changes in appearance are called its "*phases.*" The moon turns on its axis once each time it goes round the earth. Only one side of it is ever seen by us.

When the moon passes between us and the sun, as it does once a month, its dark side is turned toward us; then it gives us no light. It seems as if it had gone out, or had ceased to exist. But in a day or two a little of its bright side is turned towards us, and it appears like a strip of gold an inch broad, tapered at the ends into two sharp horns. Then it is called *new moon.*

From that time, for two weeks, it shows more of its bright side each night, till it appears round as a cart wheel. Then it is called *full moon*. From the day on which it is full until the next new moon, it seems to waste away again to nothing. Then it passes on, and begins again to enlarge as before. This is the way it does the whole year through, and from age to age.

Now, though it *appears* as if it had wasted to nothing, and an entirely new moon had come into existence, it is not so. We have the same moon now that shone upon the Patriarchs before the flood.

The moon, by its attraction, raises the tides in the ocean. But we do not know that it exerts any influence upon either the animal or the vegetable world.

LESSON CV.

GRATEFUL DEVOTION.

How much is mercy Thy delight,
    Thou ever blessed God!
How dear Thy servants in Thy sight,
    How precious is their blood!

How happy all Thy servants are,
    How great Thy grace to me!
My life which Thou hast made Thy care,
    Lord, I devote to Thee.

The soft or open sound of *ng* is heard in the following words:

bang	hang	sing	string
bring	sang	song	strong
bung	hung	sung	slung
king	ring	swing	sling
cling	ling	sprung	spring
clung	pang	tung	sprang
lungs	prong	thing	ding
rung	bung	dung	strung
stung	flung	*wring*	gang
wrong	twang	swang	gong

Although no other letter comes between the *g* and the *n* in the following words, yet they belong to different syllables; and therefore the sound proper of each, when separate, is retained:

sig nal	in dig nant	des ig na tion
sig ni fy	in dig ni ty	im preg na ble
dig ni ty	as sig na tion	sig nif i cant
dig ni fy	res ig na tion	sig ni fi ca tion
preg nant	op pug nan cy	lig num vi tæ
im preg nate	re pug nant	lig nif er ous
preg nan cy	re pug nan cy	cog ni tion
be nig nant	mag ni fy	cog na tion
be nig ni ty	mag nif i cent	ag ni tion
ma lig ni ty	cog ni zance	ig ni tion
ma lig nant	rec og nize	cog nos ci ble

"CONSIDER THE LILIES."

1. Several important lessons might be learned from a proper consideration of the lily. It is the emblem of purity, modesty and humility; and its teachings are at once pleasing and impressive.

2. In common with many other plants, it displays the wisdom, power, goodness and superintending care of the Creator. But it would seem that its *chief mission into the world was to impress upon mankind the importance of that crowning christian grace—*humility.*

3. It teaches this lesson by the *position* in which it grows, and the *attitude* which it assumes. It is "*the lily of the valley.*" It loves lonely places and lonely situations. The back-ground and the shade are its delight.

4. You do not find it on the mountain top, or showing forth its splendor from the lofty cliff. You must search for it in the most retired places. Its stalk is uncomely, and it grows without the slightest pretension. Its chief beauty is in its flowers; but it, in a great measure, conceals its leaves.

5. It shows its humility also by its *attitude* as well as its position. When the lily is about to bloom, it hangs down its head as if it wished to conceal its beauty and withdraw from observation.

6. The pink, the rose and the proud dahlia lift up their heads, and seem to covet attention and applause. "Come, see how beautiful I am." Not so the lily. It makes no such display. On the contrary, every feature indicates modesty and humility.

7. Although "Solomon in all his glory was not arrayed like one of these," the lily has neither pride nor vanity. Thus it shows how despicable are these qualities among the dwellers upon the earth.

8. From the fact that it makes no display, but conceals its beauty, it teaches us to seek *substantial worth*, and not be captivated by beauty or external appearances alone.

Questions.—Describe the lily, and state the several lessons it teaches? Notice that the sum of the whole is, that humility is the chief christian grace, and that *worth* is before beauty.

LESSON CVI.

INFINITE EXCELLENCE.

1. O could I speak the matchless worth!
   O could I set the glories forth!
     Which in my Saviour shine,
   I'd soar and touch the heavenly strings,
   And vie with Gabriel while he sings,
     In notes almost divine.

2. I'd sing the precious blood he spilt,
   My ransom from the dreadful guilt
     Of sin and wrath divine;
   I'd sing his glorious righteousness,
   In which all-perfect heavenly dress
     My soul shall ever shine.

3. I'd sing the characters he bears,
   And all the forms of love he wears,
     Exalted on his throne;
   In loftiest songs of sweetest praise,
   I would to everlasting days
     Make all his glories known.

4. Soon the delightful day will come,
When my dear Lord will call me home,
And I shall see his face;
Then with my Saviour, Brother, Friend,
A blest eternity I'll spend,
Triumphant in his grace.

CONSCIENCE.

We cannot escape the company of our own conscience. By night and by day—in company or in solitude, it is always with us. He is wise, then, who, by always doing his duty, makes conscience a pleasant and cheering companion. But to the wicked, instead of being a bosom friend, it is a bosom fury.

Ciate and *tiate* in the following words are pronounced as if written "*shate:*"

as so ciate	ex pa tiate	an nun ciate
dis so ciate	ne go tiate	li cen tiate
con so ciate	in gra tiate	sub stan tiate
e ma ciate	in sa tiate	pro pi tiate

In the following words *w* is silent:

*w*ho	*w*hoop	whom so ever
*w*hose	wholly	whole sale
*w*hom	who ever	whole some
*w*hole	who so ever	whole some ness

X, in the following words, takes the sound of *gz:*

ex ist	ex is tence	ex am ine
ex act	ex u ber ant	ex am ple
ex empt	ex hib it	ex or dium
ex hort	ex or bi tant	ex em plar
ex ert	ex ec u tor	ex em pla ry
ex alt	ex ec u trix	ex em pli fy
ex ude	ex as per ate	ex on er ate
ex haust	ex ec u tive	ex emp tion
ex ile	ex ag ger ate	ex or bi tant
ex ult	ex ot ic	ex or bi tance

LESSON CVII.

FLOWERS.

Foster the good, and thou shalt tend the flower,
    Already sown on earth;
Foster the beautiful, and every hour
    Thou call'st new flowers to birth.

Ye are the scriptures of the earth,
    Sweet flowers, fair and frail;
A sermon speaks in every bud
    That woos the summer gale.

There is a lesson in each flower,
A story in each stream and bower;
On every herb on which we tread,
Are written words, which rightly read,
Would lead you from earth's fragrant sod,
To hope, to holiness, and God.

ANTIQUATED WORDS.

Living languages are constantly changing. Certain words and phrases cease to be used; others come in their places. Words not now used are said to be *antiquated*. Many such words are now found in our translation of the sacred scriptures. The following are examples of that kind—with their meanings attached:

albeit	although	kerchiefs	caps
anon	soon	kine	cows
bewray	expose	leasing	lying
cracknels	cakes	listeth	pleaseth
days-man	umpire	let	hinder
fenced	fortified	peeled	smoothed
holpen	helped	passion	suffering
hosen	stockings	blains	blisters
molten	melted	prevent	go before
carriages	baggage	advisement	counsel
unwittingly	unawares	implead	to go to law
seethe	boil	deal	portion

strew	scatter	tache	button
twain	two	wench	gin
wist	know	sad	boiled
straitly	strictly	tale	number
meat	food	wot	knew
clean	entirely	harness	armor
quick	living	worship	reverence
ravin	prey	cunning	skillful
bruit	rumor	honest	decent
wax	become	ensue	pursue
fray	frighten	instant	earnest
eschew	avoid	trow	think

"Four beasts," living ones.
"Uppermost rooms," chief seats.
"Do you to wit," cause you to know.
"Cast in the teeth," reproach or reprove.
"Chode with," quarreled or disputed.
"Living waters," running or flowing.

LESSON CVIII.
THE TEMPTING CUP.

Look not upon the wine when it
  Is red within the cup!
Stay not for pleasure when she fills
  Her tempting beaker up!
Tho' clear its depths, and rich its glow,
A spell of madness lurks below.

They say, 'tis pleasant on the lip,
  And merry on the brain;
They say it stirs the sluggish blood,
  And dulls the tooth of pain.
Ay! but within the glowing deeps
A stinging serpent, unseen, sleeps.

Its rosy lights will turn to fire,
  Its coolness change to thirst;
And, by its mirth, within the brain
  A sleepless worm is nursed.
There's not a bubble on the brim
That does not carry food for him.

Then dash the brimming cup aside,
And spill its purple wine;
Take not its madness to thy lip—
Let not its curse be thine.
'Tis red and rich—but grief and woe
Are hid, in those rosy depths below.

WILLIS.

Words of Five Syllables, Accented on the Second.

ap pel la to ry	im pet u ous ly	un sea son a ble
sym met ri cal ly	pre em i nent ly	im mod er ate ly
u nan i mous ly	dis pen sa to ry	un par don a ble
im meas ur a ble	de lib er ate ly	pre sumpt u ous ly
im mod er ate ly	con sid er a bly	in ef fi ca cy
de rog a to ry	ir ref ra ga ble	in ac cu ra cy
de lib er ate ly	com pul sa to ry	ex ter min a ble
in con ti nen cy	com men da to ry	ex tem po ra ry
un con quer a ble	con sec u tive ly	in el li gi ble
un rea son a ble	in ap pe ten cy	ex clam ma to ry
in com pe ten cy	re mu ner a tive	he red i ta ry
in or di nate ly	pre fig u ra tive	in her i ta ble
com par a tive ly	an nun ci a tive	in vul ner a ble
con tem po ra ry	in flam ma ble ness	in su per a ble
con ter min ous ly	in com par a bly	ac com pa ni ment
con tempt u ous ly	in sep a ra ble	il log i cal ly
com men su ra ble	in ad e qua cy	un com fort a ble
con tam in a ble	e rad i ca ble	un suf fer a ble
in im i ta ble	ex trav a gant ly	un an swer a ble
in vi o la ble	in ter mi na ble	un so ci a ble
in vul ner a ble	in cu ri ous ly	fe ro ci ous ly
in es ti ma ble	un rea son a ble	im per a tive ly
in tol er a ble	in cal cu la ble	im per ish a ble

LESSON CIX.

PRAISE AND CONFIDENCE.

1. Thro' all the changing scenes of life,
    In trouble and in joy,
   The praises of my God shall still
    My heart and tongue employ.

2. My soul shall make her boast in Him,
   And celebrate His fame;
   Come, magnify the Lord with me,
   With me exalt His name.

3. The hosts of God encamp around
   The dwellings of the just;
   Deliverance He affords to all
   Who on His succor trust.

4. O make but trial of His love,
   Experience shall decide,
   How blest are they, and only they,
   Who in His truth confide.

5. Fear Him, ye saints, and you will then
   Have nothing else to fear;
   Come, make His service your delight,
   He'll make your wants his care.

Ch, in the following words, have the sound of *k*:

Christ	chlo ride	o chre ous
chasm	mon arch	sac cha rine
chrism	an arch	brach i al
chyle	Plu tarch	chol e ra
chyme	stom ach	ca chex y
chord	chro mate	chor is ter
choir	an ar chy	syn chro mism
chrome	an cho ret	chron i cle
scheme	arch i tect	chron i cler
ache	chrys o lite	pa tri arch
loch	cat e chism	eu cha rist
school	cat e chist	och i my
ar chives	char ac ter	or ches tra
an chor	in cho ate	scho las tic al
tro chee	chol er ic	pa ro chi al
cho ral	al chem ist	me chan ic al
cho rus	al chem y	al chem ic al
cha os	lach ry mal	cha me le on
i chor	ol i garch	cha lyb e ate
sep ul cher	o chre	a nach ro nism

e poch	tech nic al	chro nom e ter
ech o	arch i tect	chi rog ra phy
chron ic	arch i trave	chi rog ra pher
chem ist	arch a ism	chro nol o gy
chris tian	arch e type	mo narch ic al
Christ mas	chrys a lid	lo gom a chy
schir rus	scho li um	the om a chy
schoon er	scho li ast	cho rog ra phy
schol ar	pol e march	syn ec do che
chol er	mach i nate	bron chot o my
sched ule	mon ar chy	cat e chet ic al
pas chal	hep tar chy	ich thy ol o gy

LESSON CX.

NATIONAL PRAYER FOR THE SOUTHERN CONFEDERACY.

(*Tune*—AMERICA.)

God bless our sunny land!
May Heaven's protecting hand
  Still guard our shore,
From foes by land and sea;
May we successful be,
From strife be ever free
  As ne'er before!

From Death, a nation's grief,
O Lord, preserve our Chief:—
  Long may he live—
His heart inspire and move
With wisdom from above,
And in a nation's love
  His power control.

May just and righteous laws
Uphold the people's cause,
  And bless the South;
Land of the martyrs' grave,
Home of the free and brave!—
On such a land we crave,
  O God, thy smile.

WARD.

In the following words of two and three syllables e before the d at the end is silent, and the d is pronounced in connection with the preceding syllable:

brib ed	pav ed	us ed	con ven ed
kill ed	roll ed	tir ed	con vey ed
call ed	seem ed	seal ed	com menc ed
warn ed	mow ed	sav ed	as sum ed
saw ed	fear ed	pain ed	de priv ed
gnaw ed	rais ed	pleas ed	sur viv ed
form ed	prais ed	drain ed	de sir ed
sow ed	liv ed	rain ed	con spir ed
soil ed	oil ed	toil ed	de form ed
coin ed	foil ed	boil ed	sub serv ed
coil ed	prowl ed	growl ed	bap tiz ed
sour ed	pour ed	frown ed	blas phem ed

D, at the end of the following words, has the sound of t:

fac ed	ask ed	im press ed	dis miss ed
lac ed	fix ed	perch ed	preach ed
bas ed	mix ed	de press ed	reach ed
gra ced	talk ed	class ed	in duc ed
pla ced	walk ed	cross ed	re duc ed
rak ed	work ed	lash ed	re lax ed
quak ed	wish ed	bark ed	em bark ed
nurs ed	class ed	dash ed	dis pers ed

THE RAINBOW AND THE COVENANT.

And God blessed Noah and his sons, and said unto them: Be fruitful and multiply and replenish the earth. Every thing that liveth shall be meat for you; even as the green herb have I given you all things.

But flesh with the life thereof, which is the blood, thereof shall ye not eat.

And surely your blood of your lives will I require; at the hand of every beast will I require it, and at the hand of man; at the hand of every man's brother will I require the life of man. Whoso sheddeth man's blood, by man shall his blood be shed.

G

And God spake unto Noah and his sons with him, saying: Behold I establish my covenant with you and your seed after you. And God said: this is the token of the covenant which I make between me and you, and every living creature that is with you, for perpetual generations.

I do set my bow in the cloud, and it shall be for a token of a covenant between me and the earth. And it shall come to pass, when I bring a cloud over the earth, that the bow shall be seen in the cloud: And I will remember my covenant, which is between me and you, and every living creature of all flesh: and the waters shall no more become a flood to destroy all flesh.

And God said unto Noah: This is the token of the covenant which I have established between me and all flesh that is upon the earth.—*Bible.*

LESSON CXI.

UNITED HEARTS.

I saw two clouds at morning
Tinged with the rising sun;
And in the dawn they floated on,
And mingled into one:
I thought that morning cloud was blest,
It moved so sweetly to the West.

I saw two summer currents
Flow smoothly to their meeting,
And join their course with silent force,
In peace each other greeting:
Calm was their course thro' banks of green,
While dimpling eddies played between.

Such be your gentle motion,
Till life's last pulse shall beat;
Like summer's beam and summer's stream,
Float on in joy to meet
A calmer sea, where storms shall cease—
A purer sky where all is peace.

MOORE.

Words of Seven Syllables, Accented on the Fifth.

per pen dic u lar i ty
an ti trin i ta ri an
in de struc ti bil i ty
in el li gi bil i ty
in di vis i bil i ty
im ma te ri al i ty
in de fen si bil i ty
in con tes ti bil i ty

im pen e tra bil i ty
ir re sist i bil i ty
im per cep ti bil i ty
in com pat i bil i ty
in di vid u al i ty
in com press i bil i ty
in com bus ti bil i ty
in con form a bil i ty

The Two following in Eight Syllables have the Accent on the Sixth:

un in tel li gi bil i ty   in com pre hen si bil i ty

THE SHOPKEEPER AND THE LAWYER.

A shopkeeper, in a certain city, sent a servant to the office of a lawyer, requesting him to lend him a book which was known to be in his library. The reply was: "I cannot lend the book, but if you will come to my office you may read all day in it."

A short time after this, the lawyer, on a cold rainy morning, sent to borrow the shopkeeper's fire-bellows. The following answer was returned: "I cannot let the bellows go out of my shop; but, as often as it suits your convenience, you may come and blow all day with it."

LESSON CXII.
BEHOLD THE LOFTY SKY.

Behold the lofty sky
  Declares its Maker, God,
And all the starry worlds on high
  Proclaim His power abroad.

The darkness and the light
  Still keep their course the same;
While night to-day, and day to-night,
  Divinely teach His name.

In every different land
  Their general voice is known;
They show the wonders of His hand,
  And orders from His throne.

THE STARRY HEAVENS.

The blue canopy above us, so thickly studded with stars, has, in all ages and countries, been contemplated with wonder and delight. To us, at the South, those brilliant orbs shine with captivating beauty.

The children, therefore, of our Southern Confederacy, should not only become well acquainted with that delightful science—astronomy—which treats of them, but they should make the starry heavens a subject of frequent and delightful contemplation.

I have already told you about the sun, the moon and the earth. I will now tell you about the stars. There are two kinds of stars. One kind consists of planets; the other of fixed stars.

The word planet means a wanderer. This name is given to those orbs which revolve around the sun as their centre of motion, because they are constantly changing their places.

There are eight principal planets. None of them has any light of its own. The earth is one of the planets; and you know that it is a dark body. The names of the planets are: Mercury, Venus, the Earth, Mars, Jupiter, Saturn, Uranus and Neptune.

Each planet has two motions—one around its own axis, and the other a progressive motion in its orbit around the sun. Each turn on its axis makes a day; and a complete revolution in its orbit makes a year.

The earth turns on its axis three hundred and sixty-five times, while it makes its yearly circuit round the sun; and that is the reason why we have that number of days and nights in our year. Those planets which have larger orbits have many more days in their year than we have in ours.

All the larger planets which revolve around the sun as their centre of motion are called *primary* planets. Those which revolve round the primary are called *secondary* planets or *moons*. The Earth has one moon, Jupiter four, Saturn seven.

The use of the moon, you know, is to give light at night to the primary planet, by reflecting upon it the light of the sun. In another lesson I will tell you about the *fixed stars*.

LESSON CXIII.

WORTH OF THE BIBLE.

The Bible! the Bible!
  More precious than gold,
The hopes and the glories
  Its pages unfold!

It speaks of salvation,
  Wide opens the door;
Its offers are free
  To the rich and the poor.

The Bible! the Bible!
  Blest volume of truth;
How sweetly it smiles
  On the season of youth!

It bids us seek early
  The " pearl of great price,"
Ere the heart is enslaved
  In the bondage of vice.

Anomalous Words.

The following words vary from all the regular modes of pronouncing the vowel sounds, as indicated in the foregoing exercises:

buoy	buoe	hic cough	hik kup
choir	kwire	i ron	i urn
cough	kof	laugh ter	laf tur
draught	draft	ma ny	men ne
laugh	laf	neph ew	nev vu
one	wun	pret ty	prit te
once	wuns	waist coat	wes kot
rouge	roozhe	ser geant	sar jant
says	sez	su gar	shu gur
said	sed	wo men	wim min
slough	sluff	a gain	a gen
tough	tuff	a gainst	a genst
trough	trof	bat teau	bat to

any	en ne	bu reau	bu ro
a pron	a purn	co quette	ko ket
bu sy	biz ze	der nier	dern yare
bu si ness	biz ness	e nough	e nuf
Col o nel	kur nel	main tain	men tane
cup board	kub burd	chor is ter	kwir is ter
flam beau	flam bo	lieu ten ant	lev ten ant
haut boy	ho boe	port man teau	port man to
hal le lu jah	hal le lu ya	roq ue laur	rok e lor
pal an quin	pal an keen	belles let tres	bel la tur

CYRUS' CROWN.—Cyrus, the Persian King, was accustomed to say that did men but know the cares he had to sustain, he thought no man would wish to wear his crown.

ALEXANDER'S TEARS.—The conquests of Alexander the Great could not satisfy him; for when he had conquered the whole of the known world, he sat down and wept because he knew of no other world to conquer.

LESSON CXIV.
THE SKY-LARK.

1. Eternal minstrel, pilgrim of the sky,
   Dost thou despise the earth where cares abound,
 Or, while thy wings aspire, are heart and eye
   Both with thy nest upon the dewy ground?
 Thy nest which thou canst drop into at will,
 Those quivering wings composed, and music still.

2. To the last point of vision, and beyond,
   Mount, daring worbler! the love prompted strain,
 'Twixt thee and thine a never-failing bond
   Thrills not the less the bosom of the plain!
 Yet might'st thou seem, proud privilege to sing,
 Independent of the leafy spring.

3. Leave to the nightingale the shady wood,
   A privacy of glorious light is thine,
 Whence thou dost pour upon the world a flood
   Of harmony, with rapture more divine!
 Type of the wise who soar, but never roam,
 True to the kindred points of heaven and home!

Quotations from other Languages.

Ad infinitum	without end
Ad valorem	according to value
Alma mater	a cherishing mother
Anglice	in English
Beau monde	the fashionable world
Bona fide	in good faith
Bon mot	a witty repartee
Bon ton	the fashion
Caput mortuum	the lifeless remains
Carte blanche	unconditional terms
Compos mentis	of sound mind
Coup de main	a bold effort
Cornu copiæ	horn of plenty
En masse	in a body
E pluribus unum	one out of many
Ex officio	by virtue of his office
Ex parte	on one side
Fac simile	exact likeness
Fille de chambre	a chambermaid
Fortiter in re	firm in action
Habeas corpus	you may have the body
In statu quo	in the same state
In toto	in the whole
Ipse dixit	he said so
Ipso facto	by the thing itself
Literatim	letter for letter
Lex talionis	the law of revenge

THE ARCHER AND HIS ARROW.

A FABLE.

An archer complained of his arrow because it did not hit the mark. "If you had directed me right I should not have failed," said the arrow.

MORAL.—We too often blame others when the fault is our own.

LESSON CXV.
THE POOR OLD LYON.
A FABLE.

A noble old lyon, worn down by age and disease, lay upon the ground, groaning away the last remains of life. But now that he was thus prostrate, the ignoble beasts commenced their taunts, their insults and abuse.

The boar, with foaming rage, assailed him with thrusts of his tusks. Next came the bull, and gored him with his horns. The wolf growled and gnashed his teeth at him. Then came the ass, spiteful and insolent, and brayed at the old monarch of the forest in a most insulting manner. Having thus ascertained that his lionship was no longer able to resent an injury, or defend himself, he ventured near and *kicked him on the forehead!* Ah! said, the dying lion, I thought it hard to be insulted, in my last moments, by the *brave;* but to be thus treated by the meanest of beasts, this is past endurance—it is a double death!

MORAL.—Only cowards insult fallen greatness. Only asses kick dead lions. The most painful of all deaths is to die by the kick of an ass!

Quotations from other Languages.

[CONTINUED.]

Memento mori	be mindful of death
Mirabile dictu	wonderful to be told
Multum in parvo	much in a little
Maximum	the greatest
Minimum	the least
Ne plus ultra	nothing beyond
Non compos mentis	not of sound mind
Pater patriæ	Father of his country
Per annum	by the year
Per diem	by the day
Prima facie	first sight, or face
Pro bono publico	for public good
Pro tempore	for the time
Quantum	how much

Quantum sufficit	enough
Quid nunc	what now
Sang froid	with indifference
Sine die	no day appointed
Sine qua non	a thing indispensable
Secumden artem	according to art
Sanctum sanctorum	the most holy place
Summum bonum	the highest good
Sub rosa	under the rose
Utile dulci	the useful with the pleasant
Versus	against
Verbatim	word for word
Via	by way of
Vice versa	on the contrary
Viva voce	with the living voice
Data	truths admitted

What is a flirt? A young lady of more beauty than sense; more accomplishments than grace of mind; more admirers than friends; more fools than wise men for attendants.

LESSON CXVI.

NOW IS THE TIME.

Remember thy Creator now,
  In these thy youthful days;
He will accept thine earliest vow,
  He loves thine earliest praise.

Remember thy Creator now,
  Seek him while he is near;
For evil days will come, when thou
  Shalt find no comfort here.

Remember thy Creator now,
  His willing servant be;
Then when thy head in death shall bow,
  He will remember thee.

G*

Almighty God! our hearts incline,
Thy heavenly voice to hear;
Let all our future days be Thine,
Devoted to Thy fear.

Exercises in Spelling, Deriving and Combining Words.

Base, basely, baseness; abase, abasement; debase, debasement.

Beauty, beautiful, beauteous, beautifully, beautifulness, beauteousness, beautify.

Bounty, bountiful, bountifully, bounteous, bounteousness, bountifulness.

Form, formless, formation, formative; inform, conform, informal, conformably, conformity, conformableness, nonconformist, reform, reformation, perform, performance, informution.

Govern, governor, governess, government, ungovernable.

Honor, honorable, honorably, honorary; dishonor, dishonorable, dishonorably.

Grace, graceful, gracefulness, gracefully; ungraceful, disgraceful, disgracefully.

Credit, creditable, creditably, creditor, accredit, incredible, incredibility, discredit, creed, credence, credibility.

Cover, covering, coverlet, uncover, discover, discovery, discoverable, recover, recovery, irrecoverable, irrecoverably, irrecoverableness.

Scribe, scribble, ascribe, ascription, describe, description, inscribe, inscription, proscribe, proscription, subscribe, subscription, conscript, conscription, superscribe, superscription, descriptive, indescribable, prescribe, prescription, prescriptive.

Light, lightly, lightning, lightness, lightsome.

Season, seasoning, unseasonable, unseasonably, unseasonableness.

Venture, venturesome, venturous, venturesomeness, peradventure.

Will, willing, willingly, willingness, unwilling, unwillingly, unwillingness.

Youth, youthful, youthfully, youthfulness.

Note.—It is earnestly recommended that other similar exercises be frequently given to pupils in all our schools.

LESSON CXVII.

VOICE OF NATURE.

There seems a voice in every gale,
   A tongue in every opening flower,
Which tells, O God, the wondrous tale
   Of thy indulgence, love and power.

The birds that rise on quivering wing,
   Appear to hymn their Maker's praise,
And all the mingled sounds of spring
   To Thee a general anthem raise.

MRS. OPIE.

ARTICULATION.

By this is meant a clear, full and distinct utterance of the sound of each syllable of the words which we pronounce. You need not be told that it is a prime quality, both of conversation and of public speaking.

There is a charm about fine articulation, which captivates every ear and delights every heart. But there is a vulgarity about indistinct and slovenly utterances which is at once disgusting and painful to all persons of refined taste. How often do we hear the word "perfect" pronounced as if written *perfec!* It is robbery outright

    Thus to wrest away a *t*,
    And make it end in *c*.

The word imagination is also pronounced 'mag'nation! And you wonder what newly discovered "nation" the speaker is about to describe. But should you resent such an offense against "ears polite," the quack who uttered it will apply to you *bisters*, instead of blister, to draw upon your ill humors.

Your neighbor b'leeves he owes you for makin' his mill w'eel, and he 'sposes you 'ave no 'jections to 'ceive the money now. A pompous wight, number three, 'nounces ph'los'phers fools, and threatens to *wip* them into their senses. A fourth saw a large 'sembly last night, and he and a gem'man *talk'in* pol'tics. A fifth fought in the mem'rable battle of 'Nassas. A sixth *swan* the river Mis'sipi in Jan'wary. A seventh has the 'eadache from heatin 'ot hoysters for supper. An eighth thinks buf"los orrid hugly han'mals. A ninth took a 'slution of pep'mint for the 'sturbance of his stomach. A tenth speaks by 'thority. An eleventh prefers 'stron'my to math'matics!

LESSON CXVIII.

THE VICTORS.

I see them on their winding way,
About their ranks the moon beams play;
Their lofty deeds and daring high,
Blend with the notes of victory;
And waving arms and banners bright,
Are glancing in the mellow light.

Articulation.

[CONTINUED.]

In a previous lesson numerous examples were given of gross and ludicrous departures from the established laws of articulation. Verily such horrid butchery of our noble mother tongue is an iniquity to be punished by the judges. Not only does it greatly offend the ear, but it makes one's flesh creep to think of such barbarity. We most sincerely hope that no youth of this Confederacy will ever be guilty of such outrages against propriety and refinement.

We would, therefore, as the only sure preventive, urge upon all pupils, at the very commencement of their education, the great importance of a clear and distinct utterance of every syllable in each lesson which they either spell or read.

Form your organs of speech to proper utterances while they are tender and flexible. Learn the correct pronunciation of every word you spell or speak, and then confirm yourselves in it by daily practice.

Examples in Articulation.

armedst	harmedst	burnedst	turnedst
boastest	roastest	breakest	quakest
fouledst	howledst	talkedst	walkedst
hunteth	grunteth	laughedst	quaffedst
drinketh	thinketh	smugglest	strugglest

grantedst	hauntedst	manglest	stranglest
gain'st	rain'st	hedged	wedged
muzzledst	puzzledst	nervedst	swervedst
combedst	thwartedst	nestledst	bristledest
baskest	maskest	humblest	stumblest
drivledst	grovledst	hurt'st	dart'st
blankets	trinkets	length	strength
rapp'st	nipp'st	dipp'st	ripp'st
harpedst	carpedst	swivels	drivels
crumple	rumple	mumble	stumble
wharf'd	scarf'd	scraped	draped
whirlest	curlest	prancest	princes
rank'st	sink'st	thoughtest	boughtest
sackedst	thwachedst	wrinkledst	twinkledst
truckledst	wrongedst	strength'nest	length'nest

LESSON CXIX.

THE BEST GUIDE.

How precious is the book Divine,
  By inspiration given!
Bright as a lamp its doctrines shine,
  To guide our souls to heaven.

It sweetly cheers our drooping hearts,
  In this dark vale of tears;
Life, light and joy it still imparts,
  And quells our rising fears.

This lamp, through all the tedious night
  Of life, shall guide our way,
Till we behold the clearer light
  Of an eternal day.

THE TEN COMMANDMENTS.

The Lord our Maker has given to us His holy law as the guide of our conduct. Some of His commands are intended to restrain men's passions, and keep them from evil. Others are given to direct in the performance of duty.

Taken all together, they tell us what we ought to do, and what we must not do. How thankful should we be for such a law! Without it, how could we know what is right and what is wrong?

That law was delivered from the flaming summit of Mount Sinai, amidst the most wonderful displays of the power, majesty and glory of God. Children and all other persons should, then, have the most profound reverence for that holy law, and keep it constantly before their minds as the rule of life.

It is found in the Bible, at the twentieth chapter of Exodus. You can there read each commandment just as it was at first given. But I will here give the substance of them in a much shorter form, and happy will it be for you if you obey them:

1. Thou shalt have no more Gods but me.
2. Before no idol bow thy knee.
3. Take not the name of God in vain.
4. Nor dare the Sabbath day profane.
5. Give both thy parents honor due.
6. Take heed that thou no murder do.
7. Abstain from words and deeds unclean.
8. Nor steal, though thou art poor and mean.
9. Nor make a wilful lie, nor love it.
10. What is thy neighbor's do not covet.

Questions.—By whom was the Divine law given? Where? To whom? How many commandments? What is the first? The second? The third, &c? In what part of the Bible are they found?

LESSON CXX.

BRIGHT SIDES.

1. Whate'er the grief that dims our eye,
 Whate'er the cause of sorrow,
 We turn us to the weeping sky,
 And say, "We'll smile to-morrow."

2. And when from those we love, we part,
 From hope, comfort borrow,
 And whisper to our aching heart,
 "We'll meet again to-morrow."

THE IBEX.

1. This is quite a pretty animal of the goat kind. My young readers would all like to see it. It is nimble like

the deer, but climbs like the goat. It frequents the highest mountains, and is found chiefly in the Alps, the Caucasian Mountains, and in the mountains of Abysinia, in Africa.

2. The ibex is very shy. It retires from the haunts of mankind, and, like the chamois, it not only takes up its abode among the lofty and dreary fastnesses of the rocks, but it delights in the regions of perpetual snow; and, like the reindeer, feeds principally upon the mosses and the leaves of the dwarf shrubbery found in such regions.

3. The horns of the ibex are of enormous size. They project backward from the upper part of the crown of the head in nearly a straight direction, and then, toward the ends, curve over toward the back of the animal, extending sometimes more than three feet in length.

4. The color of the ibex changes with the seasons, from a reddish brown in summer to a brown gray in winter. This animal is hunted both for its flesh and its skin. But such is its shyness, its activity, and the extreme acuteness of its senses, both of hearing and of smell, that it is seldom taken by the most skillful hunters.

5. When tamed, they become very familiar with their owners, but nothing can tempt them to come in sight of a stranger. The ibex is equally agile and strong, and when driven to desperation, it turns upon its pursuers, and by a plunge with its powerful horns hurls them over the most dangerous precipices.

6. Hunters when thus pursued have endeavored to make their horned enemy the victim by throwing themselves flat upon the edge of a precipice, and causing the ibex to pitch headlong to immense depths below. But to their great surprise they have found that in going over it hurled itself upon its enormous horns in such a way as to escape unhurt.

Questions.—What is said of the ibex? Where found? Its haunts? Its horns? Its color? Hunted for what? Easily taken? Tamed? Fights? Leap a precipice unhurt? How?

LESSON CXXI.
NUMBERS.

Romans, bound in mental fetters,
Instead of *figures* used their letters;
For *one* an I, for *five* a V,
But X for *ten* you always see.

The L a note of *fifty* paid,
And C a hundred always made;
D, richer, for *five hundred* stood,
But M made his plump *thousand* good.

I, left of V, its value takes;
I, right, a greater value makes;
Just so, if found with X it be,
So, too, the X with L or C.

LETTERS.	FIGURES.	VALUES.
I	1	one
II	2	two
III	3	three
IV	4	four
V	5	five
VI	6	six
VII	7	seven
VIII	8	eight
IX	9	nine
X	10	ten
XI	11	eleven
XII	12	twelve
XIII	13	thirteen
XIV	14	fourteen
XV	15	fifteen
XVI	16	sixteen
XVII	17	seventeen
XVIII	18	eighteen
XIX	19	nineteen
XX	20	twenty
XXX	30	thirty
XL	40	forty
L	50	fifty

LX	60	sixty
LXX	70	seventy
LXXX	80	eighty
XC	90	ninety
C	100	one hundred
CC	200	two hundred
CCC	300	three hundred
CCCC	400	four hundred
D	500	five hundred
DC	600	six hundred
DCC	700	seven hundred
DCCC	800	eight hundred
DCCCC	900	nine hundred
M	1000	one thousand

MDCCCLXIV.

LESSON CXXII.

ONE FAMILY.

Come, let us join our friends above,
    Who have obtained the prize,
And on the eagle wings of love,
    To joy celestial rise.

Let saints below, in concert sing,
    With those to glory gone;
For all the servants of our King,
    In heaven and earth are one.

One family, we dwell in Him!
    One church, above, beneath;
Tho' now divided by the stream—
    The narrow stream of death.

One army of the living God,
    To His command we bow;
Part of the host have cross'd the flood,
    And part are crossing now.

E'en now to their eternal home
    Some happy spirits fly;
And we are to the margin come,
    And soon expect to die.

O, Savior! be our constant guide,
Then when the word is given,
Bid Jordan's narrow stream divide,
And land us safe in heaven.

C. WESLEY.

GRACEFULNESS.

Be graceful in your manners. The same thing said or done delights or disgusts hearers and observers, just in proportion as it is accompanied or deserted by good manners.

From your own observation, reflect what a disagreeable impression an awkward address, a slovenly figure, an ungraceful manner of speaking, whether, stammering, muttering or drawling, make upon you at first sight in strangers, and how lasting is the prejudice thus created against them.

PROVERBS.

Provide for the worst; the best will save itself.
Procrastination is the thief of time.
Praise the sea, but keep on land.
Politics make strange bed fellows.
Passion, like fever, leaves us weaker.
People who live in glass houses dread stones.
Possession is nine points of the law.
Promise little, but perform much.
Pull hair by hair, the scalp grows bare.
Quick resentment brings long repentance.
Raise no more spirits than you can conjure down.
Respect your promises and others will respect you.
Stop the leaks before the rain begins.
Seek the devil and you are sure to find him.
Time and Tide wait for no man.
Wishing seldom cures want.

LESSON CXXIII.

PRAISE FOR CREATION AND PROVIDENCE

I sing the Almighty power of God,
That made the mountains rise,
That spread the flowing seas abroad,
And built the lofty skies.

I sing the wisdom that ordained
  The sun to rule the day;
The moon shines full at His command,
  And all the stars obey.

I sing the goodness of the Lord,
  That filled the earth with food;
He formed the creatures with His word,
  And then pronounced them good.

Lord, how Thy wonders are displayed,
  Wher'er I turn my eye!
If I survey the ground I tread,
  Or gaze upon the sky!

THE FIXED STARS.

At first sight the stars all appear alike, and you would suppose they were all of the same kind. It is not so. The fixed stars differ from the planets; first, in shining by their own light; secondly, by their having a flickering, or flame-like appearance, while the planets shine with a steady light; and thirdly, in their retaining, at all times, the same position in regard to each other.

They all seem to move from East to West, but they all go together. It is not so with the planets. They are constantly changing their position, both as regards each other and the fixed stars.

In consequence of the earth's turning on its axis, from West to East, we are carried forward under the heavenly bodies. That makes them appear to move toward the West; but fixed stars retain the same position toward each other as the letters on a show-bill or the spots on a bed-quilt do when drawn upon the carpet.

The fixed stars are very numerous, and they are very distant from us. They may be immensely large bodies; but their great distance makes them appear very small. They shine by their own light. They are, therefore, suns. And we infer that each one is a centre of a system of worlds like ours—they revolving round, and receiving from it light and heat as we do from the central orb of our solar system. If so, how immense must be the extent of the Creator's works!

The fixed stars are divided into classes. A few of the largest form the first class. The next in size form the second class, and so down to the seventh—the smallest that can be seen without a telescope.

Groups of stars are called constellations. A noted example of this kind is what we call the "seven stars." There are very many constellations. Names have been given to them, and they are well known to astronomers and navigators. Truly, "the heavens declare the glory of God, and the firmament showeth His handy work."

LESSON CXXIV.

SAYINGS.

Quarrels would never last long, if the fault were on one side only.

Learning, with virtue, is better than houses and lands.

Difficulties are only the occasions for the development of talents.

The laws of most nations punish crimes. Those of China do more—they reward virtue.

Refrain from bitter words. There is a difference of only one letter between words and swords.

The credit that is gained by a lie lasts only till the truth comes out.

It is better to correct one fault in ourselves than to find a hundred in our neighbors.

Words of like pronunciation, but different Orthography and Meaning:

ark, a vessel	led, did lead
arc, of a circle	lead, a metal
bin, for corn	plum, fruit
been, has been	plumb, a weight
bell, to ring	ring, a circle
belle, a young lady	wring, to twist
but, a conjunction	rude, rough
butt, a large vessel	rood, of land
bred, brought up	rest, repose
bread, food	wrest, to force

sell, to dispose of
cell, a hut or cave
gilt, with gold
guilt, sin
herd, a drove
heard, did hear
him, that man
hymn, a sacred song
hart, a deer
heart, seat of life
in, within
inn, a tavern
kill, to slay
kiln, for brick
all, every one
awl, an instrument
aught, anything
ought, bound to do
hall, a large room
haul, to drag

rung, did ring
wrung, twisted
ruff, a ruffle
rough, uneven
sent, did send
cent, a coin
sum, the whole
some, a part
sun, source of light
son, a male child
too, likewise
two, twice one
ball, a round body
bawl, to cry aloud
call, to name
caul, part of the body
cord, a small rope
chord, in music
naught, bad
nought, nothing

SPICES.

Swift somewhere makes it a query whether churches are not dormitories for the living as well as the dead.

Hannah Moore says the world contains but two evils—sin and bile.

The Turks, notwithstanding the "conscientious moods" of their verbs, are said to be full of deception, and much given to lying. Beware of too much use of "indefinite tenses."

LESSON CXXV.
THE SABBATH DAY.

Oh, welcome to the weary earth,
　The Sabbath resting comes,
Gathering the sons of toil and care
　Back to their peaceful homes;

And like a portal to the skies,
  Opens the house of God,
Where all who seek may come and learn
  The way the Savior trod.

But holier to the wanderer seems
  The Sabbath on the deep,
When on and on, in ceaseless course,
  The toiling bark must keep.

And not a trace of man appears
  Amid the wilderness
Of waters—then it comes like dove
  Direct from heaven to bless.

Words of like pronunciation, but different Orthography and Meaning.

cask, a barrel
casque, armor
dam, mother of beasts
damn, to condemn.
dram, of liquor
drachm, a weight
jam, to conserve
jamb, of a door
berry, a fruit
bury, to inter
lessen, to make less
lesson, instruction
succor, help
sucker, a twig
pensile, hanging
pencil, a brush
rigor, severity
rigger, a mechanic
alter, to change
altar, for offering
augur, a soothsayer
auger, an instrument
manner, form

rap, a blow
wrap, to fold
tax, a rate
tacks, small nails
bow, to bend
bough, a branch
flour, fine meal
flower, a blossom
foul, filthy
fowl, a bird
seller, a salesman
cellar, room below
cousin, a relation
cozen, to cheat
signet, of a seal
cygnet, young swan
sealing, fixing a seal
ceiling, of a wall
vial, a bottle
viol, an instrument
cannon, a gun
canon, a rule
choler, rage

manor, lordship · collar, of a garment
pallet, a bed · profit, gain
pallette, painter's board · prophet, foreteller
mantle, garment · assent, agreement
mantel, chimney-piece · ascent, steepness

COMPLAISANCE.

If we wish the good will and esteem of our acquaintances, our good breeding must be active, cheerful and winning.

Answer in a pleasant and cheerful manner when spoken to. Do not sit while others stand. Do everything with an air of benevolent delight—not with a sour look and an indifferent manner as if you did it unwillingly.

LESSON CXXVI.

OVERDOING.

A Chinese being asked how his countrymen would express the phrase "Overdoing a business," replied: "By a hunchback making a bow."

THE MUSKET.

A son of "Green Erin" being asked whether he had ever known anything about a certain musket that was in dispute, replied: Faith, yes; I've known it ever since it was a *pistol*.

Words of like pronunciation, but different Orthography and Meaning.

ere, before · blue, a color
heir, inheritor · blew, did blow
bare, naked · bore, to make a hole
bear, to suffer · boar, a beast
beet, a root · bale, a package
beat, to strike · bail, surety
beer, a liquor · bay, of the ocean
bier, for the dead · Bey, Turkish officer
bow, to shoot with · borne, carried
beau, a gay fellow · bourn, boundary

coarse, not fine
course, direction
cote, a sheepfold
coat, a garment
fare, food
fair, beautiful
fain, gladly
feign, to pretend
grate, for coals
great, large
hare, an animal
hair, of the head
hue, color
hew, to cut
hole, a cavity
whole, entire
meat, food
meet, to assemble
mete, measure
leaf, of a plant
lief, willingly
lone, single
loan, lent
mean, low
mien, manner

core, the heart
corps, a body of soldiers
deer, an animal
dear, costly
flee, to run away
flea, an insect
freeze, to congeal
frieze, in architecture
frieze, coarse cloth
heel, of the foot
heal, to cure
here, in this place
hear, to hearken
high, lofty
hie, to hasten
I, myself
eye, organ of sight
key, an instrument
quay, a wharf
leek, a root
leak, to run out
lyre, a harp
liar, one who tells lies
moan, to lament
mown, cut down

LESSON CXXVII.

ANECDOTES.

A little boy having often heard of the *Green* Mountains, and thinking it strange that they continued so long in that condition, enquired of his father how long it would be till those mountains were *ripe*.

A splendid organ was once placed in a newly erected church. A Quaker, who had heard its rich tones with great delight, said to the pastor of the church: "Friend William, as it is thy wont to praise God by machinery, I rejoice with thee that thou hast so fine an instrument wherewith to do so!"

Words of like pronunciation, but different Orthography and Meaning.

nave, of a wheel
knave, a dishonest man
new, not old
knew, did know
pare, to cut off
pair, a couple
pear, a fruit
place, situation
plaice, a fish
raze, to demolish
raise, to lift up
rain, falling drops
reign, to rule
rein, of a bridle
sale, selling
sail, of a ship
seen, beheld
scene, of a play
see, to behold
sea, the ocean
slow, tardy
sloe, a fruit
sole, of the foot
soul, the spirit
stile, steps
style, language
strait, narrow
straight, not crooked
slay, to kill
sley, of a loom
sleigh, a vehicle
vane, a weather guide
vain, worthless
vein, for the blood
week, seven days
weak, feeble

ore, metal
oar, a paddle
pane, of glass
pain, suffering
peace, quietude
piece, a part
peer, a nobleman
pier, a column
pray, to beseech
prey, plunder
plate, a dish
plait, a fold
rye, corn
wry, crooked
rite, ceremony
write, to form letters
wright, a workman
sow, to scatter
sew, with a needle
slight, to despise
sleight, dexterity
sore, an ulcer
soar, to rise
steel, a metal
steal, to pilfer
tale, a story
tail, the end
toe, of the foot
tow, to drag
vale, a valley
veil, a covering
waste, to spend
waist, of the body
you, yourself
yew, a tree

H

LESSON CXXVIII.

THE RAINBOW.

Triumphal arch, that fill'st the sky,
  When storms prepare to part,
I ask not proud philosophy
  To tell me what thou art.

Still seem as to my childhood's sight,
  A midway station given,
For happy spirits to alight,
  Betwixt the earth and heaven.

Words which nearly resemble each other in Sound, but differ both in their Orthography and their Meaning:

air, atmosphere
are, plural of is
accept, to receive
except, to take out
affect, to move
effect, to perform
accede, to agree
exceed, to surpass
acre, a piece of land
achor, a scald head
access, approach
excess, what is over
allusion, reference
illusion, deception
elusion, escape
acts, deeds
axe, a tool
assay, to test
essay, attempt
affusion, pouring on
effusion, pouring out
allowed, permitted
aloud, with a noise
errand, a message

elicit, to draw out
illicit, unlawful
earn, to deserve
urn, vessel for remains
emerge, to come out
immerge, to plunge
fat, obese
vat, a tub
gesture, motion
jester, a joker
harsh, severe
hash, fine meat
idle, not busy
idol, a false god
impostor, a deceiver
imposture, deception
naughty, bad
knotty, full of knots
ingenuous, frank
ingenious, having skill
morse, the sea horse
moss, lichen
line, a cord
loin, part of the body

errant, wandering
addition, act of adding
edition, act of publishing
ballad, a song
ballot, a vote
creak, to make a noise
creek, a stream
clothes, garments
close, the end
consort, husband or wife
concert, harmony
descent, falling
dissent, to disagree
decease, death
disease, sickness
dost, thou dost
dust, fine powder

loom, for weaving
loam, earth
medal, a coin
meddle, to interpose
pint, half a quart
point, sharp end
radish, a root
reddish, slightly red
since, after, in time
sense, faculty or feeling
tenor, course continued
tenure, holding
talents, endowments
talons, claws
valley, space between hills
value, worth of a thing

LESSON CXXIX.

ANECDOTES.

A gentleman, whose name was "Rice," married a lady by the name of "Bacon." An editor having announced their marriage, thus gave vent to his rhyme:

> "What strange, fantastic, airy whims,
> By different folks are taken;
> She sups upon a dish of "Rice,"
> While he prefers the "Bacon."

They tell of a man down East, who is so much opposed to capital punishment that he refuses to hang his gate.

A Western farmer, it is said, declines raising poultry, lest he should get "hen-pecked."

TABLES OF SUFFIXES.

Primitive words are those which cannot be reduced to any simpler form in our language: *Teach, write, learn.*

Suffixes are letters or syllables appended to certain words to vary their force, form, and signification.

FUL, at the end of a word, means *full of*, or *abounding in:* Mirth, mirthful; health, healthful; hurt, hurtful; hate, hateful; guile, guileful; right, rightful; care, careful.

LESS, the opposite of *ful*, denotes *destitution* or *want:* Art, artless; guilt, guiltless; sense, senseless; track, trackless.

ISH denotes *likeness*, or somewhat like: Brute, brutish; white, whitish; clown, clownish; boor, boorish.

EN, as a suffix, implies *made of*, or to make: Hard, harden; soft, soften; black, blacken; oak, oaken; beech, beechen; gold, gólden; flax, flaxen.

REJOICE IN THE LORD.

Although the fig tree shall not blossom, neither shall there be fruit in the vines, the labor of the olive shall fail, and the fields shall yield no meat; the flock shall be cut off from the fold, and there shall be no herd in the stalls, yet will I rejoice in the Lord; I will joy in the God of my salvation. *Bible.*

LESSON CXXX.

MAY, FLORA AND SPRING.

Hail, bounteous May, that dost inspire
Mirth, youth and warm desire;
Woods and groves are of thy dressing,
Hill and dale do boast thy blessing.

How Flora decks the fields,
With all her tapestry! and the choristers
Of every grove chaunt carols! mirth is come
To visit mortals. Everything is blythe,
  Jocund and jovial.

Come, gentle spring, ethereal mildness, come,
And from the bosom of yon dropping cloud,
While music wakes around, veil'd in a shower
Of shadowing roses, on our plains descend.

Tables of Suffixes.

ER, OR, IST, STER, EE and ESS mean the person who, or the thing which. Ess is used to denote females only:

Vend, vender; visit, visiter; team, teamster; priest, priestess; lion, lioness; art, artist; grant, grantor, grantee; debt, debtor.

LY denotes *like*, or *in a manner:* Man, manly; wise, wisely; king, kingly; deaf, deafly; mean, meanly; scholar, scholarly; grave, gravely.

ED denotes what is done to a person or thing: Wound, wounded; sound, sounded; fold, folded; call, called; delight, delighted; end, ended.

NESS denotes the abstract quality of, or the state of: Good, goodness; bad, badness; white, whiteness; rude, rudeness; blue, blueness; swift, swiftness.

BLE, ABLE and IBLE denote capacity of, or fitness, or worthiness of: Value, valuable; blame, blameable; commend, commendable; desire, desirable; warrant, warrantable; resist, resistible; contempt, contemptible.

IC, AL and ICAL denote pertaining to, relating to, or like: Angel, angelical; method, methodical; prophet, prophetic, prophetical; poet, poetic, poetical; synod, synodic, synodical.

LESSON CXXXI.

FILIAL DEVOTION.

Some feelings are to mortals given,
With less of earth in them than heaven;
And if there be a human tear,
From passion's dross refined and clear,
A tear so limpid and so meek,
It would not stain an angel's cheek,
'Tis that which pious fathers shed
Upon a duteous daughter's head.

Tables of Suffixes.

ION and MENT express the *state of,* the *act of,* or *result of:* Relate, relation; create, creation; conclude, conclusion; state, statement; reduce, reduction; amend, amendment; subject, subjection; atone, atonement.

IZE signifies *to make, to cause,* or *to assimilate:* Brute, brutalize; legal, legalize; Pagan, Paganize; christian, christianize; idol, idolize; signal, signalize; canon, canonize.

Fy signifies *to make* or *become:* Amplify, to make ample; fructify, to make fruitful; classify, to form into classes; verify, to make known the truth.

Note.—Ing and ation are often added to words ending in fy; the former denoting *continuance*, and the latter *the act of*, or *state of:* Amplify, amplifying, amplification; multiply, multiplying, multiplication; rectify, rectifying, rectification; solidify, solidifying, solidification.

LESSON CXXXI.

FILIAL DEVOTION.

Some feelings are to mortals given,
With less of earth in them than heaven;
And if there be a human tear,
From passions dross refined and clear,
A tear so limpid and so meek,
It would not stain an angel's cheek,
'Tis that which pious fathers shed
Upon a duteous daughter's head.

Tables of Suffixes.

Ion and ment express the *state of*, the *act of*, or *result of:* Relate, relation; create, creation; conclude, conclusion; state, statement; reduce, reduction; amend, amendment; subject, subjection; atone, atonement.

Ize signifies *to make, to cause,* or *to assimilate:* Brute, brutalize; legal, legalize; Pagan, Paganize; Christian, Christianize; idol, idolize; signal, signalize; canon, canonize.

Fy signifies *to make,* or *become:*. Amplify, to make ample; fructify, to make fruitful; classify, to form into classes; verify, to make known the truth.

Note.—Ing and ation are often added to words ending in fy—the former denoting *continuance*, and the latter *the act of*, or *state of:* Amplify, amplifying, amplification; multiply, multiplying, multiplification; rectify, rectifying, rectification; solidify, solidifying, solidification.

Ance, ence, ancy, ency denote the *act of*, *state of*, or the *thing which*, or *person who:* Annoy, annoyance; abhor, abhorrence; disturb, disturbance; emerge, emergency; connive, connivance; expect, expectancy.

Note.—ANT and ENT commonly denote the *person who*, or the *thing which:* Defendant, one who defends; dependent, one who depends upon something else; absorbent, that which absorbs; corroborant, that which corroborates.

TIVE and SIVE imply *tendency to,* or *nature of:* Restorative, tending to restore; abusive, having the nature of abuse; creative, power or tendency to create; expansive, tending to expand.

ORY, TORY and SORY denote *nature of, place of, power of:* Prohibitory, power of prohibiting; laudatory, tending to, or having the nature of laudation or praise; depository, place of depositing; dispensatory, place of dispensing; observatory, place of watch or observation.

The best physicians are Dr. Diet, Dr. Quiet and Dr. Merryman.

LESSON CXXXII.

GOD'S KINGDOM.

1. The Lord Jehovah reigns,
   And royal state maintains,
   His head with awful glories crowned;
   Arrayed in robes of light,
   Begirt with sovereign might,
   And rays of majesty around.

2. Upheld by Thy commands,
   The world securely stands,
   And skies and stars obey Thy word;
   Thy throne was fixed on high
   Ere stars adorned the sky;
   Eternal is Thy kingdom, Lord!

SOLITUDE.

O sacred solitude! Divine retreat!
Choice of the prudent! envy of the great!
By the pure stream, or in the waving shade,
We court fair wisdom, that celestial maid:
The genuine offspring of her loved embrace—
Strangers on earth—are innocence and peace.

Tables of Suffixes.

Cy and ity denote state or condition, quality or capacity: Solid, solidity; calid, calidity; able, ability; ductile, ductility; sterile, sterility; accurate, accuracy; competent, competency; urgent, urgency.

Ous denotes like, partaking of, or full of: Peril, perilous; danger, dangerous; fury, furious; ruin, ruinous; venom, venomous; valor, valorous; pomp, pompous.

Bility and bleness denote the property or quality of, capacity, susceptibility or fitness: Compress, compressibility; change, changeableness; conform, conformability; diffuse, diffusableness; desire, desirableness.

Hood, ship and age denote office, state, rank or condition: Man, manhood; boy, boyhood; friend, friendship; scholar, scholarship; lord, lordship; pupil, pupilage; vassal, vassalage; waste, wastage; cord, cordage.

READING.

Boys! read something useful every day—something to reflect upon and talk about while you are at work, or as you pass along the road. Be observant. Notice everything. Converse with the wise and the good. Store your minds early in youth with wisdom. Crowd in a little every day. Neglect not the Bible. It is the only true chart of life. The ways of that wisdom which it teaches are ways of pleasantness, and all her paths are peace.

LESSON CXXXIII.

SLANDER.

A whisper woke the air—
A soft, light tone and low,
Yet barbed with shame and woe—
Now might it only perish there,
Nor farther go!

Ah, me! a quick and eager ear
Caught up the little meaning sound!
Another voice has breathed it clear,
And so it wanders round
From ear to lip—from lip to ear—
Until it reached a gentle heart,
And *that—it broke!*

Tables of Prefixes.

Prefixes are letters, syllables or words placed *before* other words to vary their form, and change or modify their signification: · Place, *mis*place; true, *un*true; believe, *dis*believe; form, *con*form.

UN is negative, and denotes *not*, or the *opposite of*, that which was before affirmed: Like, unlike; able, unable; willing, unwilling; pleasant, unpleasant.

MIS means *wrong, erroneous* or *ill:* Use, misuse; spend, misspend; rule, misrule; lay, mislay; take, mistake; name, misname.

PRE denotes *before:* Suppose, presuppose; engage, pre-engage; conceive, preconceive; meditate, premeditate; examine, pre-examine; dispose, predisposed.

RE implies *again, back* or *repetition:* Write, rewrite; compose, recompose; unite; reunite; construct, reconstruct; place, replace; imburse, reimburse.

E, EX, EF and EC are the same. They mean *out, out of, from:* Educe [from duco I lead and e out] means to lead or draw out; elope, to run away; expel, to drive away; effuse, to pour out; extirpate, to root out; eclectic, chosen out; extract, to draw out.

IM, IN, IL and IR have the same meaning—that of *destitution* or *want:* Proper, improper; pure, impure; secure, insecure; complete, incomplete; legal, illegal; logical, illogical; regular, irregular; resistible, irresistible.

DI, DIS and DIF have the same meaning—*assunder, separation, division:* Join, disjoin; agree, disagree; robe, disrobe; fuse, diffuse; divide, [*video* I see, and *di* asunder] separate into parts; differ [*fero*, I bear or carry, and *di* or *dis* asunder] to be wide apart, or very unlike; use, disuse; like, dislike; form, difform.

A narrow-minded person has not a single thought beyond he little sphere of his own vision. The snail, says the Hindoo, sees nothing but his own shell, and thinks it the grandest palace in the universe.

H*

LESSON CXXXIV.
HONEY AND FLIES.
A FABLE.

Honey was poured out in a wide dish. Flies were enticed by it. But having lit upon it, they sank down into it, became entangled, and could no more escape.

"How cruel," said one of them, "is this flattering sweet! It first *entices*, then *kills*." So with all sinful pleasures.

Tables of Prefixes.

COL, COM, CON, CO, COR, are only different forms of *con*, together; and they mean *with, together, jointure, union:* Heir, coheir; press, compress; mingle, commingle; locate, collocate; migrate, commigrate; relative, correlative; partner, co-partner.

AD means *to*, and from it are formed AC, AF, AL, AN, AP, AS, AT, all of which mean *to:* Adjoin, admit, affix, ally, annex, affy, anoint, appoint, assent, assort, attune, attach, accept, accrue, accord.

IN takes the form of IM, IL, IR, the general meaning of which is *in* or *upon:* Press, impress; come, income; impose, imprint, insult, induce, infuse, inflame, inhale, illude, illume, irrode.

Note.—IN sometimes implies *negation:* Irregular, not regular; irresistible, not to be resisted.

BI means *two* or *double:* Biform, bicornous, bisect, biangular, bicorporal, bimanous, biennial, biped, bivalve.

INTER means *between:* Intermix, interleave, interlink, intervene, interweave, intermarry, interline, intermeddle, intercept, interchange, interjacent.

TRANS and ULTRA mean *over* or *beyond:* Transalpine, transmarine, transatlantic, translucent, transgress, transpose, transmit, transcend, transform, translate, ultra mundane, ultra mural, ultra marine.

UNSAFE.—A sea-captain declared in relation to a fast sailing belle of the upper ten grade, who was glittering with gorgeous silks and costly jewelry, "It is an unsafe vessel where the rigging is worth more than the hull."

SLEEP.

Oh! lightly, lightly tread!
A holy thing is sleep,
On the worn spirit shed,
And eyes that wake to weep!

* * * * * *

Tired nature's sweet restorer, balmy sleep!
He, like the world, his ready visit pays
Where fortune smiles; the wretched he forsakes;
Swift on his downy pinion flies from woe,
And lights on lids unsullied with a tear.

Tables of Prefixes.

PRO means *before, forth* or *forward:* Procure, proceed, produce, provide, provoke, progression, propelling, progenitor.

PER means *through, by, thoroughly,* or *by means of:* Perchance, per day, pervade, perform, perfect, permit, persuade, perjure, perforate, persecute.

MONO means *one:* Monocular, monogram, monosyllable, monochromatic, monomania, monologue.

POLY means *many:* Polysyllable, polyglot, polytheism, polyanthus, polypede, polymorphous.

OMNI, PAN and PANTO mean *all:* Omniscient, omnipresent, omnipotent, omnivorous, omniferous, panoply, pantomime.

UNI means *one:* Uniform, univalve, univocal, universe, unison, unanimous.

MULTI means *many:* Multiform, multiangular, multinominal, multifarious, multilateral.

EQUI means *equal:* Equidistant, equiangular, equinox, equiponderate, equivocal, equiform, equivalent.

ANTI means *against:* Antichrist, antifebrile, antipodes, anticontagious, antimonarchical.

EM and EN mean *in* or *into*. They also intensify: Embitter, enhance, enrich, entrap, enmesh, enwrap, entangle, ensure, enchain, embolden, empower, ensnare.

DEMI, HEMI and SEMI mean *half:* Demigod, demi-man, demidevil, hemisphere, semitone, semilunar, semicircle, semiannual.

TRI means *three:* Triangle, triform, tripod, triennial.

NOT A DUST HOLE.—A gentleman opened his snuff-box, and, holding it out to his friend, politely invited him to take a pinch of snuff. To this the other replied: "No, I thank you, sir; my Maker never made my nose for a *dust hole*, or he would not have turned it wrong end up.

LESSON CXXXVI.
THE SOLDIER.

How beautiful in death
  The warrior's corse appears,
Embalm'd by fond affection's breath,
  And bathed in woman's tears.

Give me the death of those
  Who for their country die;
And oh! be mine like their repose,
  When cold and low they lie!

Their loveliest mother earth
  Enshrines the fallen brave,
In her sweet lap who gave them birth,
  They find their tranquil grave.

Tables of Prefixes.

SUPER, SUPRA and SUR mean *over, beyond, upon:* Superhuman, superabound, supervene, supervise, superscribe, surpass, surmount, surcharge, survive, supravulgar, superangelic, superfine, surcingle, surtout, superadd.

SUB and SUBTER mean *under:* These change into *suc, sup* and *suf,* but retain the meaning of *sub:* Submit, submarine, subastral, sublunary, subterrene, subside, succumb, succor, support, suppose, subjugate, subterfluent.

OB means *before* or *opposite.* It changes also into *oc, of, op* and *os:* Object, oppose, occur, offer, oblige, oppugn, obligate, ostend, ostensible.

RETRO means *back:* Retrospect, retrograde.

BENE means *well:* Benevolent, beneficent, benefit, benefactor.

MAL and MALE mean *bad:* Maltreat, malpractice, malcontent, maladminister, malformation.

DE means *down, off, from:* Depress, derive, depose, denude, derange, decamp, dethrone.

CIRCUM means *round:* Circumvolve, circumfluent, circumscribe, circumpolar, circumspection, circumambient, circumference.

ANTE means *before:* Antedate, antecede, antemeridian, antemundane, antecedent.

POST means *after:* Postpone, postscript, postmeridian, posterior, postdiluvian, postmortem.

PHILIP, king of Macedon, when wrestling at the Olympic games, fell down in the sand. Having arisen, he beheld the print of his body in the place where he had fallen, and exclaimed: "O, how small a portion of earth will hold *us* when we are dead, who are ambitiously striving after the whole world while we are living!"

LESSON CXXXVII.
DEFECTIVE EDUCATION.
"PAST WRECKS GIVE FEARFUL WARNINGS."

The defects of early education are a species of "fretting leprosy," which cleaves to its subjects to the day of their death. Even when those defects are not of the most glaring character, still they are like the blighting East wind let in upon all the fair pastures of life.

To persons in prominent public stations, they occasion "deaths oft"; and, at the same time, inflict the deepest mortification upon all their admirers and friends. Take the following examples as specimens:

A pursy old gentleman, who had spelled "*dimes* and *dollars*" more frequently than any other words in the English language, proposed to a brilliant assemblage at a Governor's levee, that they should drink a toast to "The three R R R." On being asked for an explanation, he replied he meant, "*Readin, Ritin, and Rithmetic.*"

A man of mark for means and influence in his own neighborhood, informed his factors that "weynd" and "weothur" permitting, he would visit them the next week. A waggish member of the firm, on receipt of his letter, remarked: "Our old friend must recently have acquired some prodigious electrical influences, for he has raised one of the most awful *spells of weather* I have ever witnessed."

A lady who had exchanged a swamp plantation for a palace in a city, informed her friends that since she " had came " to reside in the city, she had taken quite a " *likation* " to literature.

A good old lady, who kept a public house in a certain village, having learned that an eclipse of the sun would be " *visible* " at that place, the next day, went earnestly to work, preparing for the reception of a great crowd. Inquiry for the cause of all that, was made by her neighbors. Her reply was, that the *Eclipse* was coming to town to-morrow—everybody would be there to see it, and she must prepare to accommodate as many as she could!

A miss in her advanced "teens," who boasted of spending most of her time in "readin and writin," was asked which she mostly wrote, poetry or prose: " O, na-ra one," said she, " I write *small hand!* "

A French clergyman having laid down the law of duty, strongly urged upon his congregation compliance with it on the ground of the relation subsisting between them; viz: that he was their shepherd, and they were his " muttons."

An Englishman comforted his people under sore trials by telling them that the " *harm* of the Lord " was around them for protection. Another read of the " Angle of the church," instead of the Angel.

And still another informed his auditors that he would read for their edification a portion of the Pcfsams "—that is the psalms !

LESSON CXXXVIII.

BLISS FROM SORROW.

What bliss is born of sorrow ?
'Tis never sent in vain—
The Heavenly surgeon maims to save,
He gives no needless pain.

DEFECTIVE EDUCATION.

[CONTINUED.]

A young lady of fine personal appearance, but who had more of Juno than Minerva in her composition, on being asked, in the midst of a brilliant literary circle, if she had ever read the "Last of the Mohegans," with a captivating lisp on her tongue, promptly replied: "No, sir, I never got that yet; but I read the *first* some time ago."

Many an Englishman calls for "ot hoysters," instead of hot oysters.

A planter says of his low lands: "They are very *prol-i-fiss*"—meaning prolific.

A man of great wealth ordered a "statute" of Washington to adorn his grounds.

Another denounced his factors because when he ordered a *carriage*, they bought for him a "ve-hick-kle"; and declared that no such "critter" should come upon his premises.

A certain lady has procured a portion of the "saliva" of Mount Vesuvius for her cabinet. She is very anxious also to visit the "Niagara Springs."

"Which do you admire most, Cæsar or Pompey?" said a literary savan to his domestic beauty. "That," said she, "depends on the use one has for them. Cæsar is the best field hand; but Pompey is the best cook." On receipt of this response, the learned gentleman, without waiting to witness the prowess of Cæsar as Field Marshal, or test the culinary skill of Pompey, made his own *desert* and left for parts unknown.

The Speaker of the House of Representatives, in the Legislature of one of the States, declared that if they should so disgrace humanity as to pass a bill that was then up for consideration, he would forsake civilized society and take up his abode among the "*Ab-ro-ghines*."

A fashionable lady declared that she had seen the wounded General carried off upon an "avalanche," and she heard his groans "*visibly*, quite *visibly!*"

The friends of a Governor elect of one of the States beyond the line, advised him to procure, as part of his outfit, a fine *library*—named many standard works, and then "miscellaneous" books. He replied that the first named sets of books he would procure; but as for MISS LANY'S, she might keep her's till doomsday, for he never would have in his library a book "*wrote by a woman.*"

LESSON CXXXIX.
STEADFAST HOPE.

While floating on life's troubled sea,
  By storms and tempests driven,
Hope, with her radiant finger points,
  To brighter scenes in Heaven.

She bids the storms of life to cease,
  The troubled breast be calm;
And in the wounded breast she pours
  Religion's healing balm.

Her hallowed influence cheers life's hours,
  Of sadness and of gloom;
She guides us through this vale of tears,
  To joys beyond the tomb.

DEFECTIVE EDUCATION.
[CONCLUDED.]

The preceding lessons on this subject present numerous examples of the ludicrous lights, and the utterly prostrated positions, in which certain persons have been placed—not from any mental or moral defects, but solely from the want of education.

They knew no better; and, therefore, they were to be pitied. But even pity, in such case, is no relief. It is but the testimony of the heart to the lamented fact of their ignorance, and the deep mortification it gives to their friends. Then,

  " No such pity e'er demand,
  But boldly on your merit stand."

Ignorance on the part of most children and youth in our day and country, is a sin—a grievous sin against God and man—against the highest interests also of themselves and their country.

Even now, such examples are the rare exception, not the rule. Better days for our Confederacy are at hand. The ignorant, from this period onward, will be a small and an obscure minority. *Be not ye found among them.*

Nor is it a vain boast to say, what, from personal acquaintance I know to be the fact, that the Confederate States abound in highly educated, refined and noble-minded citizens.

Our Orators, Statesmen, Judges, Generals, and other professional men, would do honor to any country. Our enemies themselves also being judges, it is an admitted fact, that in matronly dignity, elevated sentiments and refined taste, the ladies of this Confederacy are "chief among the highest."

Emulate, then, these noble examples; and avoid the solitary wrecks to which I have pointed. Be men *that are men;* women *that are women*—not *pretenders* to the name. Be worthy of your country and your expected destiny. Let your unremitting effort also be, to make your country—your own "*sunny South,*"—the model country of the world—

"The land of all the lands the best."

ABBREVIATIONS EXPLAINED.

A. A. S. Fellow of the American Academy.
A. B. Bachelor of Arts.
Abp. Archbishop.
Acct. Account.
A. D. Anno Domini, the year of our Lord.
Ala. Alabama.
A. M. Master of Arts; before noon; in the year of the world.
Apr. April.
Atty. Attorney.
Aug. August.
Bart. Baronet.
B. D. Bachelor of Divinity.
B. V. Blessed Virgin.
Bbl. Barrel.
C. Centum, a hundred.
Cant. Canticles.
Capt. Captain.
Chap. Chapter.
Col. Colonel.
Co. Company.
Com. Commissioner, Commodore.
Cr. Credit.
Cwt. Hundred weight.
Chron. Chronicles.
Cor. Corinthians.
Conn. or Ct. Connecticut.
C. S. Keeper of the Seal.
C. S. A. Confederate States of America.
C. P. S. Keeper of the Privy Seal.
C. A. S. Fellow of the Connecticut Academy.
Cl. Clerk, Clergyman.
Cons. Constable.

Gent. Gentleman.
Geo. George, Georgia.
Gov. Governor.
G. R. George, the King [of England]
H. S. S. Fellow of the Historical Society.
Heb. Hebrews.
Hon. Honorable.
Hund. Hundred.
H. B. M. His or Her Britannic Majesty.
H. C. M. His most Christian or Catholic King [of France and Spain.]
Hhd. Hogshead.
Ibid. in the same place.
i. e. that is (id est.)
id. the same.
Ind. Indiana.
Inst. Instant.
Is. Isaiah.
Jan. January.
Ja. James.
Jac. Jacob.
Josh. Joshua.
Jun. Junior.
K. King.
Km. Kingdom.
Kt. Knight.
K. C. B. Knight Commander of the Order of the Bath.
K. G. C. Knight of the Grand Cross.
K. G. Knight of the Garter.
L. C. Lower Canada.
L. or Ld. Lord or Lady.
Lev. Leviticus.
Lieut. Lieutenant.

Nov. November.
N. S. New Style.
N. W. T. North Western Territory.
N. Y. New York.
Obj. Objection.
Ob. Obedient.
Oct. October.
O. S. Old Style.
Parl. Parliament.
Pa. Penn. Pennsylvania.
Per. by; as, per yard, by the yard.
Per Cent. by the Hundred.
Pet. Peter.
Phil. Philip, Philipians.
Philom. A lover of learning.
P. M. Post Master, Afternoon.
P. O. Post Office.
P. S. Postscript.
Ps. Psalm.
Pres. President.
Prof. Professor.
Q. Question, Queen.
q. d, as if he should say.
q. l., as much as you please.
q. s. a sufficient quantity.
Regr. Register.
Rep. Representative.
Rev. Reverend, Revelation.
Rt. Hon. Right Honorable.
R. I. Rhode Island.
S. South, Shilling.
S. C. South Carolina.
St. Saint.

Cts. Cents.
D. D. Doctor of Divinity.
Dea. Deacon.
Dec. December.
Del. Delaware.
Dept. Deputy.
Deut. Deuteronomy.
Do. Ditto, the same.
Dr. Doctor, or Debtor
E. East.
Eccl. Ecclesiasticus.
Ed. Edition, Editor.
E. G. for example.
Eng. England, English.
Eph. Ephesians.
Esa. Esaias.
Ep. Epistle.
Esq., Esquire.
Etc., and so forth, et cœtera.
Ex. Exodus, Example.
Exr. Executor.
Feb. February.
Fr. France, French, Frances.
F. R. S. Fellow of the Royal Society, (Eng.)
Gal. Galatians.
Gen. General.

Lond. London.
Lon. Longitude.
Ldp. Lordship.
Lat. Latitude.
Lou. Louisiana.
LL. D. Doctor of Laws.
lbs. Pounds.
L. S. Place of the Seal.
M. Marquis, Meridian.
Maj. Major.
Mass. Massachusetts
Math. Mathematics.
M. B. Bachelor of Physic or Medicine.
Matt. Matthew.
M. D. Doctor of Physic.
Md. Maryland.
Me. Maine.
Mr. Master, Sir.
Messrs. Gentlemen, Sirs.
MS. Manuscript.
MSS. Manuscripts.
Mrs. Mistress.
N. North.
N. B. Take Notice.
N. C. North Carolina.
N. H. New Hampshire.
N. J. New Jersey.
No. Number.

Sect. Section.
Sen. Senator, Senior.
Sept. September.
Servt. Servant.
S. T. P. Professor of Theology.
S. T. D. Doctor of Divinity.
ss. to wit, namely.
Surg. Surgeon.
Tenn. Tennessee.
Theo. Theophilus.
Thess. Thessalonians
Tho. Thomas.
U. C. Upper Canada.
Ult. the last, or the last month.
U. S. A. United States of America.
V. Vide, See.
Va. Virginia.
viz. to wit, namely.
Vt. Vermont.
Wt. Weight.
Wm. William.
Wp. Worship.
Yd. Yard.
& And.
&c., And so forth.

PUNCTUATION.

Punctuation is the division of a composition into sentences or parts of a sentence by points, to mark the pauses to be observed in reading, and show the connection of the several parts or clauses.

The comma (,) indicates a pause of the length of a monosyllable, or the time of pronouncing *one*. The semicolon (;) indicates a pause of two monosyllables; a colon (:) of three; a period (.) four. The period is placed at the close of a sentence.

The interrogation point (?) denotes that a question is asked, as, *what do you see?*

An exclamation point (!) denotes wonder, astonishment, or other emotion, expressed by the foregoing words.

A parenthesis ( ) includes words not necessary in the sentence, and which are to be uttered in a lower tone of voice.

Brackets or hooks [ ] are sometimes used for nearly the same purpose as the parenthesis, or to include some explanation.

A dash (—) denotes a sudden stop or a change of subject, and requires a pause, but of no definite length.

A caret (ʌ) shows the omission of a word or letter, thus, give me *the* book.

An apostrophe (') denotes the omission of a letter or letters, thus, lov'd, tho't.

A quotation is indicated by these points, " " placed at the beginning and end of the passage.

The index (☞) points to a passage which is to be particularly noticed.

The paragraph (¶) denotes the beginning of a new subject.

The star or asterisk (*), the dagger (†) and other marks (‡. §. ‖), and sometimes letters and figures, are used to refer the reader to notes in the margin.

The diaresis (¨) denotes that the vowel under it is not connected with the preceding vowel.

CAPITAL LETTERS.

A capital letter should be used at the beginning of a book, chapter, section, sentence and note. It should begin all proper names of persons, cities, towns, villages, seas, rivers, mountains, lakes, ships, &c. It should begin every line of poetry, a quotation, and often an important word.

The name or appellation of God, Jehovah, Christ, Messiah, &c., should begin with a capital.

The pronoun I and interjection O are always capitals.

TESTIMONIALS IN FAVOR OF THIS WORK.

While on a visit to his highly valued friend, Col. W. Perroneau Finley, late President of Charleston College, whose judgment and taste in literature, and whose zeal in the cause of education are well known, the Author requested of him a review and criticism of the manuscripts of The Confederate Spelling Book, before committing it to press. That service he rendered in connection with his friend and pastor, the Rev. John R. Dow, of Aiken, S. C., and the following paper was returned as their opinion of its merits:

AIKEN, S. C., Oct. 27, 1863.

The Rev. Washington Baird, being about to publish, for the use of schools in the Confederate States, a Spelling Book, interspersed with Reading Lessons in prose and poetry, &c., and having explained to us the system on which it has been prepared, and having submitted many portions of the manuscripts containing lessons adapted to the various stages of a pupil's progress, we take pleasure in now expressing our opinion of the merits of his work.

We consider this book of Mr. Baird's, not only a great desideratum in our schools, but, as the title page asserts, well calculated to please and instruct the young; and while it imparts useful information, its tendency is to produce correct moral impressions.

It has also the special merit of being adapted to our Southern latitude, and in accordance with the views and sentiments of the people of the Confederate States. We also think it a valuable acquisition as a family book for the instruction and training of children during their elementary course; and we have no hesitation in recommending it to the patronage of all who are concerned or interested, either professionally or otherwise, in the training of the young and rising generation. We really think, also, that Mr. Baird deserves the gratitude of the Southern people for this elaborate, well-timed and patriotic contribution to the mental and moral furniture of our schools, and the educational resources of our country.

W. PERRONEAU FINLEY,
JOHN R. DOW.

The following persons, distinguished for their position, their attainments, and their profound interest in the cause of education, have also united in their commendation of this work to the confidence and patronage of the public—some of them from a thorough examination of the manuscripts, and all of them from accurate knowledge of its character, designs and merits.

J. L. REYNOLDS, D. D.,
Prof. of Roman Literature in South Carolina College, and Editor of the Confederate Baptist, Columbia, S. C.

JAMES C. FURMAN, D. D.,
President of the Furman University, Greenville, S. C.

JAMES P. BOYCE, D. D.,
Prof. of Theology in said University.

A. M. SHIPP, D. D.,
President of Wofford College, Spartanburg, S. C.

DAVID DUNCAN,
JAMES H. CARLISLE,
WARREN Du PRE,
Professors in said College.

Col. JAMES FARROW,
Member of the Confederate Congress from South Carolina.

JOSEPH. R. WILSON, D. D.,
Pastor of the Presbyterian Church, Augusta, Ga.,

Hon. E. A. NISBET,
Col. WASHINGTON POE,
Rev. DAVID WILLS,
Macon, Ga.

Hon. G. E. THOMAS,
S. H. HIGGINS, D. D.,
Columbus, Ga.

W. STATES LEE, Esq.,
Rev. C. P. B. MARTIN,
Principals of High Schools, Columbus, Ga.

Rev. WILLIAM FLINN,
Milledgeville, Ga.

S. K. TALMAGE, D. D.,
President of Oglethorpe University, Ga.

Rev. R. C. SMITH,
Rev. C. W. LANE,
Professors in said Institution.

Hon. JOSEPH E. BROWN,
Governor of the State of Georgia.

www.ingramcontent.com/pod-product-compliance
Lightning Source LLC
Chambersburg PA
CBHW020240170426
43202CB00008B/169